NEW RULES

D1602784

NEW RULES

CALIFORNIA'S MARIJUANA LAW EXPLAINED

An Indispensable Guide for
Marijuana Consumers, Gardeners,
and Patients in California

JEREMY DAW, J.D.
with ED ROSENTHAL

NEW RULES
California's Marijuana Laws Explained

Copyright © 2017 Jeremy Daw
Published by Quick American Publishing
A division of Quick Trading Co.
Piedmont, CA

Printed in Canada
First Printing

ISBN: 978-1-936807-27-7
eISBN: 978-1-936807-37-6

Project Editor: Rolph Blythe
Editorial Assistance: Araxi Polony, Darcy Thompson
Cover Design: Kelly Winton
Interior Design: Neuwirth & Associates
Library of Congress Control Number: 2017953124

CONTENTS

CHAPTER ONE: YOUR NEW RIGHTS

CHAPTER TWO: THE LAW'S LIMITS

CHAPTER THREE: A TIME OF CHANGE

About This Book

IF YOU'RE A CALIFORNIA CANNABIS USER, MEDICAL MARI-juana patient, or ganja gardener, this book is for you. In it, I aim to demystify the intricacies of cannabis policy so you'll have a solid framework from which to make better-informed decisions.

This book focuses on consumers—both patients who need medical marijuana to treat their conditions, and responsible adults who simply enjoy it. Yet I also address Californians who *don't* like cannabis and may never try it in their lives—worried parents, for example, or neighborhood advocates. Proposition 64 was written with many groups in mind. Nearly every provision in its 62 pages represents some form of compromise between competing interests— the result of town hall–style meetings, held up and down the state in the year leading up to the election, in which the Yes on 64 campaign tried to hear everyone's concerns.

There are actually two new laws that are changing cannabis policy in the Golden State—Proposition 64, passed in 2016, and its medical equivalent, the Medical Marijuana Regulation and Safety Act, or MMRSA, passed by the state legislature in 2015. Both laws are timed to go into effect at about the same time and in many ways, were designed to work together. Yet important differences divide the two laws as well. Throughout the text of this book I will make constant reference to MMRSA in an attempt to help readers keep all the differences straight.

I can see a new, exciting legal landscape just over the next ridge of rolling golden hills. This is the map that shows the way there.

Jeremy Daw, J.D.
Berkeley, California

INTRODUCTION

Ed Rosenthal

MOST PEOPLE FAMILIAR WITH MARIJUANA RECOGNIZE that it is a benign substance that enhances their lives and a medicine with virtually no serious side effects. So people are puzzled that it took fifty years since the first anti-prohibition organization was founded* for us to enjoy legal marijuana in California.

There are many theories on why politicians have opposed it, so much so, that it took an initiative to bring even a semblance of legalization. I think that maybe when they asked the magic mirror who was more popular—any one of them, or some fine cannabis—they invariably finished second. The reason: good marijuana never told a lie.

I was not in favor of Prop. 64. I think Californians deserved a better initiative than a series of laws written by a small cabal of billionaires. However, these are the laws we have. Its most positive effect is that it will provide legal sta-

---

* LEMAR founded by Mike Aldrich at SUNY Buffalo, NY, 1967

tus and access to cannabis for all Californians over the age of twenty-one.

However, PROP 64 is not a simple law. It is a 60-page document, 12,400 words long. It was written to satisfy various stakeholders such as government officials, cops, prosecutors and tax agencies, but for the most part marijuana users are treated only as an afterthought.

This book is designed to help you negotiate the labyrinth of seemingly contradictory provisions that were not clearly thought out, written by people not familiar with marijuana or its uses.

All the people involved in *New Rules* are intimately involved in marijuana and understand the implications of the law's provisions. We also describe how it relates to MERSA, the legislation enacted in anticipation of the voters' acceptance of Prop. 64. This is especially important to medical marijuana users.

We wrote *New Rules* to keep you out of trouble, not to extract you from it. So it is important that you read it now, as the laws come into effect. Knowing what's legal is the best way to keep you from legal entanglements.

Now let's enjoy the new rules. Because they're not just new rules; it's a new game. Have a happy legalization.

Medical Use, Adult Use

ON ONE LEVEL THERE'S LITTLE DIFFERENCE BETWEEN medical marijuana and recreational cannabis. All marijuana as well as industrial hemp (also legalized by Prop. 64) are the same species, a fact attesting to the remarkable versatility of *Cannabis sativa* L. The plants themselves have no idea whether they're being grown for medical or relaxational applications, and even two strains bred for different purposes will often reveal only slight differences in the composition of their chemistries, if any at all. Most recreational users will receive certain medical benefits from using cannabis (especially if they choose it as a substitute for more dangerous drugs such as tobacco or alcohol), even if they don't know or don't care. At the same time, many medical patients derive a pleasant, relaxed feeling from taking their medicine (or, perhaps, an unpleasant, overwhelmed feeling if they take too much) that is incidental to their treatment plan. The difference between cannabis's effects and side effects is, perhaps more than that of any other drug, a matter of tautology: as Shakespeare pointed out, a rose by any other name smells just as sweet.

Yet for better or worse, the history of cannabis policy reform in the United States has decisively split the categorization of the plant's uses into two principal tracks. As a result of this history (see "How We Got Here," below), Californians now have two major cannabis laws: the Medical Marijuana Regulation and Safety Act, or MMRSA, and the Adult Use of Marijuana Act (also known as AUMA, or Proposition 64)—the *NEW RULES,* which are the subject of this book.

Attempts to legislatively divide state markets into two camps have not always gone well. While the state of Colorado won a good government award from the Brookings Institution for its successful rollout of adult use cannabis legalization in a medical marijuana market, the states of Washington and Oregon have fared worse. Lawmakers in those states discovered that teasing out the difference between patients and other consumers is not so easy, even when trying to do so in good faith—and not all efforts in these states have been in good faith (see "Ask a Patient," Chapter 3).

To ease California's transition, the state legislators who wrote MMRSA and the Yes on 64 campaign, which led to the development of AUMA, took a few cues from one another to coordinate two systems that work, in many ways, hand in hand. In general terms, MMRSA repeals the caregiver and collective system that has been the legal backbone of California's medical marijuana policy for the past 20 years and replaces it with a much more heavy-handed regulatory approach. Contrary to popular belief, California's Compassionate Use Act of 1996 (CUA, Prop. 215)—the first major medical marijuana reform in modern history—did not legalize medical marijuana, or at least not in the same way that most subsequent medical marijuana laws did. Instead, CUA (as well as the legislature's contribution to the law in 2003, known as SB 420) carved out medical exceptions to the state's criminalization of marijuana, which otherwise remained intact. Since then, state appellate courts have debated back and forth whether the exceptions these laws created are *defenses* or *immunities*, but the overall effect is about the same either way: the possession, sale, and cultivation of cannabis remain criminal activities, even while the state recognizes exceptions for qualified medical use.

Equal Opportunity?

Although MMRSA and Prop. 64 take important steps to de-escalate the drug war, this is not to say that everyone will be treated the same under the new rules.

I was one of the first to raise the alarm about the possibility that MMRSA's license application rules could be used to snatch economic opportunities from the hands of entrepreneurs in poor neighborhoods currently taking advantage of the state's ambiguous medical laws in order to hand those same opportunities to investors with less experience, but with more money and better connections.

MMRSA, working together with Prop. 64, turns this law on its head. It transforms medical marijuana from a defense in criminal court to a fully legal, fully regulated activity. Instead of making legitimate use the exception, the laws will make legality the rule—assuming that everyone is playing by the rules, that is.

In short, the medical marijuana industry is about to trade the cop for the bureaucrat (and especially the taxman). Medical marijuana will become just as legal as any other legitimate commodity—but at the same time, it will become one of the most heavily regulated of all regulated industries. Civil asset forfeiture will be traded for hefty tax bills, raids for random inspections, and helicopter flyovers for environmental protection reviews.

For consumers, these changes will have many effects, but the most important is to force a choice: to remain a "patient" or to become an "adult consumer"? I will explore this issue in greater depth in chapter three, but for readers wondering what's in a name, the punch line is: more than you may think.

MEET A CANNABIS USER

Throughout this book, we will meet a range of people whom California's new marijuana rules affect. You may find your own story here, or the story of a friend or relative. I'd encourage you to look in the back of the book for additional profiles and Q&A's with experts and industry insiders.

A Cannabis Consumer—Lonnie Marks

Lonnie is a hardworking mother of three who helps to run her family's auto shop in Sacramento. She doesn't use much cannabis but she finds that taking a few puffs helps her greatly whenever her arthritis starts acting up. Yet at the same time, she is concerned about her children, ages between 10 and 15, and worries that if they find out about her occasional cannabis use, that they may decide it's alright for them to start the kind of daily habit that could negatively affect their lives. We will hear from Californians like Lony throughout this book, to learn how the changes in cannabis law will affect them.

MEET:

A Medical Marijuana Patient—Angela Bacca

Angela was diagnosed with Crohn's disease, a painful and debilitating condition affecting the gastrointestinal system, when she was about to start her freshman year in college. As a teenager growing up in Lompoc, she had already discovered that using marijuana made her feel better but did not understand why. After her diagnosis, she learned how to use marijuana as a powerful adjunct therapy that allowed her to reduce her reliance on invasive surgeries and powerful pharmaceutical steroids, and instead maintain something close to a normal college life. Although she treated herself with marijuana on a daily basis, this treatment did not prevent her from earning a degree in journalism from San Francisco State University and an MBA from Mills College. Angela is now a resident of Oregon, and we will hear her thoughts comparing the previous medical system of California with the recreational legalization recently implemented in her new home state. See Chapter 3 for a Q&A with Angela.

FIGURE 1:
TIMELINE OF CALIFORNIA'S NEW RULES

MMRSA	PROP. 64
September 11, 2015 MMRSA passed by legislature as AB 243, SB 643, AB 266	**May 4, 2016** The Adult Use of Marijuana Act (AUMA) qualifies for state ballot
October 9, 2015 MMRSA signed into law by Governor Brown	**July 1, 2016** AUMA approved by the state voters as Proposition 64
January 1, 2016 Preferred licensees in operation before	**September 1, 2016** Preferred licensees in operation before
February 3, 2016 MMRSA "drafting error" deadline repealed	**November 9, 2016** California voters approve Prop. 64, 57 percent to 43 percent
March 1, 2016 MMRSA "drafting error" deadline, encouraging cities and to pass rush bans	**November 9, 2016** Criminal prohibitions against personal possession lifted
May 1, 2016 BMMR's first draft of medical rules released	**November 9, 2016** State opens applications to revoke criminal records
January 1, 2018 MMJ licenses begin and collective defense repealed	**January 1, 2018** First round of licenses issued
January 1, 2020 Organic standards for MMJ	**January 1, 2023** First large farms open

Map of California County Rules

NOVEMBER 2016

1. Del Norte
2. Siskiyou
3. Modoc
4. Humboldt
5. Trinity
6. Shasta
7. Lassen
8. Tehama
9. Plumas
10. Mendocino
11. Glenn
12. Butte
13. Sierra
14. Lake
15. Colusa
16. Sutter
17. Yuba
18. Nevada
19. Placer
20. Sonoma
21. Napa
22. Yolo
23. Sacramento
24. El Dorado
25. Marin
26. Solano
27. Amador
28. Alpine
29. San Francisco
30. Contra Costa
31. Alameda
32. San Joaquin
33. Calaveras
34. Tuolumne
35. Mono
36. San Mateo
37. Santa Clara
38. Stanislaus
39. Merced
40. Mariposa
41. Madera
42. Santa Cruz
43. Monterey
44. San Benito
45. Fresno
46. Inyo
47. Kings
48. Tulare
49. San Luis Obispo
50. Kern
51. San Bernardino
52. Santa Barbara
53. Ventura
54. Los Angeles
55. Orange
56. Riverside
57. San Diego
58. Imperial

	INDOOR	OUTDOOR	COMMERCIAL	MANUFACTURING
Alameda	Regulated	Regulated	Regulated	BAN
Alpine	BAN	BAN	BAN	BAN
Amador	Regulated	Regulated	BAN	BAN
Butte	Regulated	Regulated	BAN	BAN
Calaveras	Regulated	Regulated	Regulated	Regulated
Colusa	BAN	BAN	BAN	BAN
Contra Costa	BAN	BAN	BAN	BAN
Del Norte	Regulated	Regulated	BAN	BAN
El Dorado	Regulated	Regulated	Regulated	BAN
Fresno	BAN	BAN	BAN	BAN
Glenn	Regulated	Regulated	BAN	BAN
Humboldt	Regulated	Regulated	Regulated	Regulated
Imperial	Regulated	Regulated	BAN	BAN
Inyo	Regulated	Regulated	BAN	BAN
Kern	Regulated	Regulated	BAN	BAN
Kings	BAN	BAN	BAN	BAN
Lake	Regulated	Regulated	Regulated	BAN
Lassen	Regulated	Regulated	BAN	BAN
Los Angeles	Regulated	Regulated	Regulated	Regulated
Madera	Regulated	Regulated	BAN	BAN
Marin	Regulated	Regulated	Regulated	BAN
Mariposa	Regulated	Regulated	BAN	BAN
Mendocino	Regulated	Regulated	Regulated	Regulated
Merced	Regulated	Regulated	BAN	BAN
Modoc	Regulated	Regulated	BAN	BAN
Mono	Regulated	Regulated	BAN	BAN
Monterey	Regulated	Regulated	Regulated	Regulated
Napa	Regulated	Regulated	BAN	BAN
Nevada	Regulated	BAN	BAN	BAN
Orange	Regulated	Regulated	BAN	BAN
Placer	BAN	BAN	BAN	BAN
Plumas	BAN	BAN	BAN	BAN
Riverside	BAN	BAN	BAN	BAN
Sacramento	Regulated	Regulated	BAN	BAN
San Benito	Regulated	Regulated	BAN	BAN
San Bernardino	Regulated	Regulated	BAN	BAN
San Diego	Regulated	Regulated	BAN	BAN
San Francisco	Regulated	Regulated	Regulated	Regulated
San Joaquin	BAN	BAN	BAN	BAN
San Luis Obispo	Regulated	Regulated	Regulated	BAN
San Mateo	Regulated	Regulated	Regulated	BAN
Santa Barbara	BAN	BAN	BAN	BAN
Santa Clara	Regulated	Regulated	BAN	BAN
Santa Cruz	Regulated	Regulated	Regulated	Regulated
Shasta	Regulated	BAN	BAN	BAN
Sierra	Regulated	Regulated	BAN	BAN
Siskiyou	Regulated	Regulated	Regulated	BAN
Solano	Regulated	Regulated	BAN	BAN
Sonoma	Regulated	Regulated	Regulated	BAN
Stanislaus	BAN	BAN	BAN	BAN
Sutter	Regulated	BAN	BAN	BAN
Tehama	Regulated	Regulated	BAN	BAN
Trinity	Regulated	Regulated	BAN	BAN
Tulare	Regulated	Regulated	Regulated	BAN
Tuolumne	Regulated	Regulated	BAN	BAN
Ventura	Regulated	Regulated	BAN	BAN
Yolo	Regulated	Regulated	BAN	BAN
Yuba	Regulated	Regulated	Regulated	BAN

How We Got Here

While the voters and legislators of California have expanded medical marijuana rights over the past 20 years on a statewide level, California judges have, even while protecting some important patient rights, greatly increased the power of cities and counties to regulate cannabis cultivation out of existence.

This is no exaggeration. See the map in figure 1 for a showing of counties that, at the time of the vote in favor of Prop. 64 in November 2016, had passed de jure or de facto bans of personal cultivation of cannabis––even for medical use––within their jurisdictions. Most of these counties had also banned dispensaries, so while patients who lived there had a theoretical right to access their medicine under state law, local law placed great distances between them and the closest legal places to either purchase or grow it. While this may be an annoying inconvenience for healthy Californians, for patients this can mean great hardship.

This is why it is significant that Prop. 64 establishes a right to cultivate up to six cannabis plants for the personal use of all adults, statewide. In the context of the cultivation bans that have swept the state over the past decade, this represents an important step forward for patients left out in the cold.

CHAPTER ONE

Your New Rights

POSSESSION

The Adult Use of Marijuana Act (AUMA), also known by its ballot initiative number, Proposition 64, legalized the possession of small amounts of cannabis by any Californian age 21 years or older on midnight of Election Day 2016. While activists celebrated by lighting up at the momentous moment, some observers could be forgiven for wondering what the big deal was—after all, some thought, wasn't this stuff practically legal already?

Not really. Prop. 64 represents a tectonic shift of California cannabis law by turning both rules and exceptions on their heads: what was once the exception is now the rule, and vice versa.

The core of Prop. 64, now enshrined in state law as California Health and Safety Code sections 11362.1 through 11362.45, opens with these highly significant words:

> It shall be lawful under state and local law, and shall not be a violation of state or local law, for persons 21 years of age or older to:

(1) Possess, process, transport, purchase, obtain, or give away to persons 21 years of age or older without any compensation whatsoever, not more than 28.5 grams of marijuana not in the form of concentrated cannabis;

(2) Possess, process, transport, purchase, obtain, or give away to persons 21 years of age or older without any compensation whatsoever, not more than eight grams of marijuana in the form of concentrated cannabis, including as contained in marijuana products;

(3) Possess, plant, cultivate, harvest, dry, or process not more than six living marijuana plants and possess the marijuana produced by the plants;

(4) Smoke or ingest marijuana or marijuana products; and

(5) Possess, transport, purchase, obtain, use, manufacture, or give away marijuana accessories to persons 21 years of age or older without any compensation whatsoever [the "pass the joint" rule].

Prop. 64 adds:

Marijuana and marijuana products involved in any way with conduct deemed lawful by this section are not contraband nor subject to seizure, and no conduct deemed lawful by this section shall constitute the basis for detention, search, or arrest.

Why is this so important? Compare to Prop 215, the Compassionate Use Act of 1996 (CUA), California's pioneering medical marijuana law. For all the headlines that voter initiative garnered and the explosion of gardens and dispensaries that followed in its wake, the CUA never went so far. Instead of unequivocally declaring medical marijuana to be lawful, as Prop. 64 does for adult use cannabis, CUA left the criminalization of all forms of marijuana on the books. Instead of creating a new rule, it created an exception to the old one.

CUA was a bold, innovative step forward in cannabis policy. Ironically, that very reality encouraged its occasionally timid language. In 1996, no modern state had ever passed such an expansive medical marijuana reform. The drafters of CUA were boldly progressive in their broadly worded definition of what would qualify as "medical" under their law, and indeed no state since has ever enacted such a permissive definition of medical marijuana. However, the authors' believed, in part because of the boldness of CUA's definitional reforms, voters were not ready for other major changes to the cannabis laws. While leaving marijuana prohibition in place, the 1996 law carved out certain exceptions to the rules.

In 2003, the state legislature expanded medical rights with the passage of SB 420. This paved the way for the collective and cooperative system under which the majority of the state's dispensaries are now organized; but it didn't change the default criminality of cannabis—it only expanded exceptions to the criminal law. However, the difference is quite real. Unlike the old law, the new one:

▸ Prevents Child Protective Services from taking children away from parents because they were discovered in possession of medicine to treat a medical condition.

▸ Prevents a job applicant from getting turned down because he or she has a marijuana arrest on his or her record, which they were formerly required by law to disclose.

Prop. 64 moves the rights to possess and consume marijuana from an exception to a criminal rule to an unequivocal expression of legal activity. California's new rules put adult possession and consumption rights on a firmer footing. The century-old prohibition of personal cannabis possession in California has finally come to an end.

CULTIVATION

In contrast to the straightforward possession rights, which Prop. 64 grants to California adults statewide, the right of Californians to cultivate their own cannabis gardens is complex, nuanced, and depends in large part on where they live.

While Prop. 64 firmly establishes the right for adults to possess their own personal quantities of marijuana, on the matter of personal cultivation it strikes a compromise between activists who wanted to guarantee cultivation access across the state, and some conservative local cities and counties that wanted the ability to minimize cultivation in their jurisdictions. The compromise includes exceptions that, for many but not all Californians, may end up swallowing the rule.

First, a little background on how we got here. While the voters and legislators of California have expanded medical marijuana rights over the past 20 years on a statewide level, California judges have, even while protecting some

Possession— Where and How Much

Adults age 21 and over now have the right to possess marijuana statewide, but that right does not extend everywhere. Here are some of the places that will still be off-limits:

▸ Schools, parks, day care centers — anywhere you're likely to find children

▸ Jails, halfway houses — and parolees still have to abide by conditions of their parole

▸ At work, employers still have the right to set their own "drug-free" policies

▸ Tenants must still abide by landlords' nonsmoking policies

Adults are allowed to possess enough marijuana or concentrate for their personal use, which the law defines as:

▸ Up to an ounce (28.5 grams) on your person, where not prohibited (see above)

▸ Up to 8 grams of cannabis concentrate, except where prohibited

▸ The produce of your legal garden, kept secured at home

New Proposed Medical Rules

As this book was going to press, the state announced a new set of first draft rules covering many different aspects of the operations of medical marijuana licensees under MMRSA. Most of these changes will only affect license holders "behind the scenes" and won't have any direct effect on patients, but some of them may exert a strong effect indeed on California consumers.

At the time this book went to press, these rules had not yet been finalized and are thus subject to change. But they do provide a useful glimpse at the kind of thinking the state has been using when considering how to regulate the medical marijuana industry which is about to be transformed by the state's new rules:

No late-night dispensaries? The new rules propose to limit the operating hours of dispensaries to between 6:00 am and 9:00 pm, Pacific time.

New purchase limits: The rules propose to limit the amount of medicine a dispensary may sell to a patient or caregiver in a single day, to 8 ounces of flower —but this cap can be waived if the patient has a doctor's note specifying that they need more. The state has also proposed to limit the sale of concentrates to 8 grams per patient per day and to define a "dose" of edible medical marijuana as 10mg of THC and to limit the total THC in an edible package to 100mg.

No delivery by drone: Yes, they actually addressed this. The proposed rules go on to specify that medical marijuana deliveries must be made by a car with a GPS tracking system to an actual physical address —so no more back-alley deals to get your meds!

important patient rights, greatly increased the power of cities and counties to regulate cannabis cultivation out of existence (see appendix C for a listing of the major cases).

Inside or Out?

But, as with so much else with California's new rules, the right to personal gardening comes with its own caveats, the result of fine-tuned compromises. While marijuana users wanted all adults to have the right to grow their own cannabis for their own use, many local governments in California pushed back. Some local authorities resented the proliferation of ganja gardens that appeared all around the state under its lightly regulated medical laws. They were not willing to support a statewide initiative that would undo all of those local changes. Thus the language of Prop. 64 attempted to strike a balance between statewide access and local control.

One of the principal objections at city councils complained of the wafting smell of outdoor gardens and in response, many local governments declared the smell of cannabis a nuisance. In truth, the nuisance argument is overblown, especially considering that there are literally hundreds of terpenes (the organic chemicals that give most plants their smells) in cannabis, ranging from blueberry to pine and almost every scent in between—it's just illogical to paint such a diverse bouquet with the single brush of "nuisance."

In the rarer cases of would-be entrepreneurs exploiting local garden rules to run a business out of a residential area (see "Ask a Cannabis Regulator," Chapter 3), complaining neighbors had a better point. Regardless of the reasons, in the battles between patients and neighbors, the victors have been the neighbors almost every time, and the result has been a medical marijuana state with almost no place to grow marijuana (see figure 1).

Prop. 64's compromise affirms the rights of local governments to regulate personal cultivation but also prohibits them from "completely prohibit[ing] persons [from cultivating up to 6 plants] inside a private residence, or inside an accessory structure to a private residence located upon the grounds of a private residence that is fully enclosed and secure" [11362.2(b)(2)].

This essentially gives the green light to any city or county government that wants to ban all outdoor gardens, while preserving the right of adults who want to grow to do so—as long as they keep their gardens inside their home or greenhouse. Unfortunately, while this choice is good for neighbors who don't want to look at a marijuana garden next door, it is terrible for the planet—growing cannabis indoors has a much larger carbon footprint than letting it grow under the sun, where the plant can pretty much take care of itself.

It is an imperfect compromise to be sure, but the theory is that what is out of sight (and smell) is out of mind. Further, this power does not extend until the end of time; when the federal government finally lifts its prohibitions on marijuana, the power of local governments in California to ban all outdoor gardens will be repealed too.

Prop. 64's win was a decisive victory at the state level but far more battles have been fought at local ballots, where the patchwork of victories and losses—on both sides—has painted a far different picture. One typical battleground is Calaveras County, where a citizen initiative to ban commercial cannabis activity was filed, sued by activists for misleading language, removed by a judge, filed again, then sued again, and finally removed. Then voters and local government worked together to approve a bill to regulate the activity instead. And this is just one example of many local struggles ranging throughout the whole length of the state.

While Prop. 64 and MMRSA do much to find compromise between consumer access and skittish local governments, these battles remain far from resolved. Indeed, local power struggles have not been so much eliminated by California's new laws, as redefined. Once again one of the principal fronts will be the ballot box: Prop. 64 allows the kind of commercial ban that was so contentiously fought in Calaveras County, but only when the ban is approved by the vote of the local residents. So rather than put these matters definitively to rest, California's new laws will probably provoke a flurry of local ballot battles—at least in the short run.

Vaping and e-cigs

Unfortunately, Prop. 64 reflects the same policy insanity that has currently gripped Sacramento concerning the regulation of electronic cigarettes. Despite research conducted right here, at the University of California, showing that the "smoke" from a marijuana vaporizer can be up to 95 percent cleaner than that from a joint, Prop. 64—like California's laws concerning the consumption of tobacco—treats e-cigs and vaporizers exactly the same as joints and pipes. This is insane. California's laws should encourage smokers, of any substance, to choose the safer product for both themselves and those around them. But Prop. 64 treats the inhalation of clean cannabis vapor and dirty joint smoke as if they were identical.

THE LANDLORD EXCEPTION

But there's one other important exception to the right for California adults to grow their own cannabis: the right of landlords to put the kibosh on the idea. As Prop. 64 makes explicit [sec. 11362.45(h)], none of the rights of consumers to possess, use or cultivate cannabis will infringe on *"the ability of an individual or private entity to prohibit or restrict any of the actions or conduct otherwise permitted...on the individual's or entity's privately owned property."* As with so many other California laws, this rule favors the landed gentry. A similar principle permits employers to ban the possession and use of cannabis on the premises of their workplaces (see "Patient FAQ," Chapter 3).

Thus in the final analysis, on the matter of personal cultivation, Prop. 64 exchanges one set of compromises for another. Before its passage, patients had the right to cultivate their own medicine (either themselves or with the help of a caretaker), but only if they were lucky enough to live in one of the counties or cities that hadn't passed a cultivation ban. With the new law's passage, all adults over age 21 have the right to cultivate up to six plants statewide, but only if they are lucky enough to afford a greenhouse or indoor setup, and only if they are fortunate enough to either own their own home or to have a landlord who allows a small garden. Some Californians will live in a city or county that permits more than the statewide minimum number of plants and doesn't vote to ban outdoor gardens. In these special zones, it will really look (and smell) like legalization!

First, Prop. 64 empowers cities and counties to "regulate" personal cultivation, with the caveat that such regulations must be "reasonable." Of course, you might immediately realize that reasonable is in the eye of the beholder, and that some judges might think it reasonable to allow city councils to automatically reinstate their old cultivation bans without so much as consulting the voters. Yet there are already legal limits on what can actually qualify as reasonable local cultivation regulations.

One is a line of cases, already well developed in areas of law that apply to non-marijuana businesses, about what kinds of local regulations are reasonable. For example, it's reasonable to limit the opening hours of a bar that sells alcohol so that raucous drinkers don't keep the bar's neighbors up all night, but a local ordinance limiting a bar's hours only to between 9:30 and 11:00 on Tuesday mornings would be an unreasonable regulation, amounting to a de facto ban.

CONSUMPTION

Like its rules concerning personal cultivation, Prop. 64's rules on consumption hinge greatly on where you live—yet there are some principles that apply everywhere in the state.

The rules on smoking cannabis will be familiar to anyone who knows California's rules for smoking cigarettes. Basically, anywhere it's illegal to smoke tobacco, it will most likely be illegal to smoke marijuana too. That means parks, schools, and most private places of business. So generally, when we're talking about inhaling cannabis, we mean the same rules as for cigarettes—but there are important differences.

Penalty List

It's legal to drive a car in California, but driving too fast risks a traffic ticket. A similar principle applies to the consumption of marijuana under Prop. 64, except that some of the penalties are a lot worse than a traffic ticket! Make sure to avoid breaking these consumption rules so you don't risk a fine, or worse.

Smoking in public	$100 fine
Smoking where smoking tobacco is prohibited	$250 fine
Open container in a car, boat or plane.	$250 fine
Smoking at a school or day care center while children are present	up to $500 fine and/or 6 months in jail!

HASH AT HOME?

Unfortunately, one rule that isn't different from the rules for tobacco pertains to Californians who rent their home. Generally, landlords are free to set restrictions on the smoking of tobacco in their apartments as part of their lease—they can charge a cleaning fee or deposit for smoking inside, and they can even require their tenants to go outside and smoke on the porch or balcony. Prop. 64 sets a similar rule for the smoking of cannabis, and you can expect any landlord who imposes rules on the smoking of cigarettes on their property to impose similar rules for marijuana too. This comes with two caveats, though. One is that this rule only applies to *nonmedical* use of cannabis—the laws regulating the rights of California *patients* to medicate in their own home are more complicated (see "Patient FAQ," Chapter 3). The other caveat is more practical: given that landlords are forbidden from barging in on their tenants with less than 24 hours' notice, and given that the smell from marijuana vaporizers can dissipate within minutes—this is particularly tough to enforce.

When in a school zone or any other area within 1,000 feet of a school, day care or youth center, you'll have to be extra careful. There, no smoking will be allowed if there are minors present, and even if you happen to live within 1,000 feet of a school and you're just toking up at home, the new rules will require you to keep your smoking "not detectable by others on the grounds" of the protected area. So sitting on your front porch and blowing bong-rip smoke rings at the middle schoolers on their way to class is inviting trouble! Indeed, the law might even be read as unfairly discriminating against responsible adults who live near schools, since they will be held to a higher standard for keeping the smell of their legal activity out of children's noses. For these Californians, they'll need to keep it extra discreet, even if it is legal.

CANNABIS IN THE CAR?

While the rules of smoking cannabis or tobacco in the home are similar, when it comes to driving in your car the rules are very different. When it comes to your car, the analogy is much closer to alcohol—YOU CAN'T SMOKE WHILE DRIVING, and even having an "open container" of pot in your car is still against the law. Tobacco-using Californians are free to smoke cigarettes because of a medical consensus that nicotine does not render its users unsafe to drive. But for adults who choose marijuana instead, the law is clear in its expectations: that you'll pick up your pot at the store and keep it in a closed container all the way home.

But what exactly is an "open container," anyway? In the case of alcohol, the distinction is quite obvious to any traffic cop: it's quite clear if a can of beer or a bottle of wine has been opened. But marijuana often comes in a resealable container like a baggie, and without any roaches in the ashtray it may not be immediately obvious that a driver has been improperly consuming pot in the car.

This doesn't mean that it will be impossible for police to do their jobs. If a cop suspects that drivers or passengers have been using cannabis in a car, they can look at the label on whatever cannabis container they find to determine how much it originally contained. If they weigh it and find that there is some missing, they will consider the container an open one and ticket the driver. In addition, many packages sold in California have tamper-evident seals, which makes investigation even easier. But not all marijuana will be required to be kept in such a container under the new rules, so this remains a gray area that will have to be clarified in the future.

The bottom line is that it's legal to drive to a dispensary or retail store to buy cannabis under these laws, but once it's purchased the only safe move is to leave the product in the bag until you get home.

Amsterdam
on the Boardwalk

As with California adults who want to grow their own marijuana, the luck of Californians who want a convenient place to consume it varies from place to place. For adults in conservative jurisdictions who live close to a school, for example, the legal landscape will look a whole lot like prohibition from the vantage of their bedroom closet, blinds drawn, and smoke filtered through a tube of toilet paper with a napkin of fabric softener wrapped over one end. But the really lucky ones will hit the legalization jackpot.

While Prop. 64 generally restricts the smoking of cannabis to the home and away from schools and youth centers, it leaves open space for local governments, if they so choose, to license businesses for on-site consumption. This means that Amsterdam-style "coffee shops" are coming to California! They will only be permitted in cities that vote to allow them, and you can expect all kinds of regulations that will dictate air filtration, careful separation of the smoking room from areas visible (or smellable) by the public, and forbidding businesses with liquor licenses (e.g., bars) from selling pot too. But this is still a big deal—soon, some lucky Californians will have a choice of inviting their friends out to the hash bar instead yet another night out drinking alcohol. When the first coffee shop opens its doors on the California beach, it will finally feel like real legalization.

WEED AT WORK?

Another big difference is at the workplace. Under Prop. 64 and in California law generally, employers are free to set their own policies about the consumption of substances on their workplace grounds. Generally, employers are tolerant of tobacco smoke breaks, but if you're caught doing shots of tequila on the clock, you'll probably have a chat with HR in your future. Because the impairment potential of marijuana is closer to that of alcohol than that of cigarettes, you can expect that most employers will ban the smoking of cannabis by employees on the grounds—and under Prop. 64, they're allowed to do it.

This rule applies to adult use of cannabis. The rules concerning the rights of medical cannabis patients to use marijuana, and the tension those rights create with the right of employers to maintain "drug-free workplaces" is much more complex. For more information, see "Cannabis in the Workplace," Chapter 2 and "Patient FAQ," Chapter 3.

WHERE TO GET IT

Many California cannabis consumers get most of their supply from a dispensary or delivery service. These collectives will operate under tighter regulations. However, consumers will not find the differences to be that obvious. In sum, consumers will have the same basic options available to them as they have now, but with more choices, some of which will come with new taxes.

As California undergoes its transition from a medical to a hybrid system with recreational and medical economies existing side by side, consumers will face the choice of remaining patients in the medical system or making a jump to the adult consumer rules under Prop. 64.

The authors of Prop. 64 seem to have anticipated that most will choose to become adult consumers. The goal of Prop. 64 is to add to, not replace, the current medical system, but for the two systems to exist successfully side by side, a significant number of cannabis consumers will need to shed their patient status and make the jump.

In other states that have both medical and recreational legalization, the transition has not always been smooth. In Oregon, which legalized medical marijuana in 1998 and recreational marijuana in 2014, a large disparity in taxes created incentives for legislators to defy the will of voters and launch attacks against the state's patients. Medical marijuana was not taxed, but recreational supplies were taxed at 25 percent, which incentivized consumers to try to remain patients. The state government, missing out on the tax money it wanted for other programs, encouraged patients to become adult consumers and now the majority of the system is categorized under the much more tax-lucrative recreational system. (See "Ask a Patient," Chapter 3). Now the state is looking at further consolidation—operating all marijuana programs under a single agency.

California's legislature moved preemptively. Anticipating the possibility that recreational legalization could pass in 2016, Sacramento passed a comprehensive medical mar-

Organic Standards

One of the features Prop. 64 provides for adult consumers is a directive to the California Department of Food and Agriculture to develop an official California organic standard for cannabis similar to the organic standards for other products grown in the state.

Of course, organic cannabis is already plentiful in California, if you have the right connections. But this standard, if thoughtfully drafted, will increase consumer confidence in the cleanliness of their marijuana products. Currently, independent testing laboratories provide most of the quality assurance for California cannabis, and the state's most-professional labs have plenty of experience detecting the presence of pesticides and other chemicals that would violate quality standards. In all probability Food & Ag Department will enlist the state's licensed laboratories to be their frontline partners in enforcing quality standards for both organic and nonorganic products

ijuana regulation bill—MMRSA—in 2015 (see Introduction); this bill included the controversial move of imposing high taxes on the state's medical marijuana supplies, which had been previously taxed on the local level only. The taxes subsequently imposed on recreational supplies by Prop. 64 are almost identical to MMRSA's taxes on medical supplies, so if the system works as intended there should be little difference in price between patients and other consumers. While this has the advantage of discouraging government officials from trying to eliminate the state's medical program, California's patients will have to pay a steep price for it.

DELIVERY SERVICES

Delivery services, whether collectives that offer to bring cannabis to your door or software apps, such as Meadow, that help you find them, are already a well-established corner of California's cannabis scene.

Currently, delivery services operate in a legal gray area. The Compassionate Use Act of 1996, the state's first medical marijuana law, didn't explicitly authorize the delivery of marijuana, but a state court later ruled that the right to transport medical marijuana was implied by the law's other provisions. The state's subsequent collective law, SB 420, made the legality of the state's medical collectives official, but didn't explicitly address delivery services either.

Now delivery collectives stand with one foot on the legislature-created right to form medical collectives and one foot on the judge-created right to transport medicine to patients—but it's not clearly defined or regulated by either area of law (see also "Patient FAQ," Chapter 3).

Prop. 64 and its medical cousin, MMRSA, changes this. The collective model is being eliminated for both medical and recreational delivery services. Instead, a new system based on state-issued licenses will divide the transportation sector in half: one license will be for consumer *delivery*, the other for industry transport.

Consumer delivery will be similar to a retail store license. The latter license to *transport* cannabis applies only to licensees who move the products from farm to distributor and from distributor to retailer. While this system will help the government to track cannabis supplies and maintain quality control, one likely effect will be to drive up the purchasing cost for consumers (see "The Price of Pot," Chapter 3).

Safety on the Roads

Drunk driving has long been one of the most tragic and senseless causes of death in the United States, so it's quite understandable that many Californians are concerned about the effect of marijuana legalization on the safety of the state's roads. The subject has been hotly debated on all sides, with legalization advocates pointing out that marijuana impairment is less dangerous behind the wheel than drunkenness and opponents asking why encouraging increased consumption of any intoxicant is a good thing.

On this question, the early data from Colorado has been mixed. On the one hand, the Colorado Department of Public Safety's statistics show no significant increases in traffic accidents in the years after the commercialization of medical marijuana there in 2010 or after the state's vote to legalize adult use in 2012. But on the other hand, there has been a recent increase in fatal traffic accidents in the state, and especially those in which DUIs have been involved.

Yet even this is not necessarily an effect of marijuana legalization, as marijuana intoxication alone contributes little to the state's total DUI statistics (see "Ask a Cannabis Regulator," Chapter 1).

This experience agrees with the latest science, which has clarified that marijuana intoxication is less of a threat to safe driving than previously thought. Rogeberg and Elvik (2016) found that "acute cannabis intoxication is associated with a statistically significant increase in motor vehicle crash risk... of low to medium magnitude" because of compensation strategies used by stoned drivers to lower their risk. This is a tendency that drunk drivers tragically lack, which is why their risk of accident is much greater than that of their stoned counterparts. So while the risk of driving under the influence of marijuana is significant, it pales in comparison to drunk driving—and there may even be an argument to try to encourage adults to try marijuana *instead* of alcohol, if one accepts that there are situations in which drivers are going to drive impaired regardless. Reasonable minds can disagree.

Of much greater concern is the possibility that Colorado drivers might be combining alcohol and marijuana together to become more dangerous to other drivers than they would be on either substance alone. It's still too early to say whether legalization is helping or hurting in this regard, but this is an important issue to watch for California.

MICROBUSINESSES AND NONPROFITS

Besides regulating retail options that already existed, Prop. 64 also pioneers new ways for consumers to find cannabis as well as possibly reinvigorating an old model that was popular in the early years of medical marijuana but has languished since.

Prop. 64 sets up an innovative new model called a microbusiness. Along with the green light for on-site consumption, this will be one of the principal features that sets California's law apart from other states.

Prop. 64 and MMRSA replace the state's current collective system with a new regulated system based on licenses for every stage of the cannabis industry. However, many patients appreciate the state's collective system and the intimate relationship it fosters between farmer and consumer. They feared that the new license system, which placed the state in the middle of every transaction from farmer to distributor to retailer to consumer, would destroy the community culture that the collective system fostered.

The microbusiness model was designed to ameliorate that effect by preserving the collective feel of small operations that would prefer to break down the barriers between farmers and the consumers they serve. With this versatile option, farms with less than 10,000 square feet of canopy under cultivation can farm cannabis, process and manufacture it into edibles or extract, transport it to market, and even sell it directly to consumers all under one license. Amidst a regulatory system that otherwise tries to put an all-knowing state at the helm of every transaction, think of the microbusiness license as the small business safety valve.

The other noteworthy retail option is a return to California's cannabis roots. Some of the state's earliest medical marijuana operations were patient nonprofits that were funded by donations or sliding-scale payments from patients. The images broadcast by mainstream media outlets, showing suffering patients finding succor at the hands of charitable operations, helped to shape the positive national image that medical marijuana continues to enjoy today.

Prop. 64 attempts to continue this tradition by empowering the state and local governments to license cannabis-distribution nonprofits and to create special tax and professional incentives to encourage their success. However, these steps are optional.

It's up to the state or local governments to allow the return of the nonprofit system. It would be a tremendous aid to patients, many of whom will struggle to pay all the new taxes created by the state's new laws. This is the spirit in which California first led the charge to reform cannabis laws, showing a great example for the other 49 states to follow.

Dan Rowland works for the city of Denver, Colorado, where one of his primary duties has been to help implement the legalization of cannabis in a responsible way. As the first state to pass full cannabis legalization in the US—or indeed the world—Colorado has become an important bellwether for states like California to watch. The city of Denver has embraced the state's legalization law more fully than any other jurisdiction, so it is no exaggeration to say that Dan's office sits atop the epicenter of marijuana legalization worldwide.

I caught up with him to ask how legalization is going, focusing in particular on the three issues that may concern Californians more than any others—the effects of legalization on crime rates, road safety, and the use (and abuse) of cannabis among adolescents.

Q: After the commercialization of medical marijuana in Colorado in 2010 and adult use legalization in 2014, what has been the effect of the marijuana industry on Denver's crime rates?

A: Less than half of a percent of Denver's overall crime is attributable to the marijuana industry. However, we see a lot of burglaries committed against the industry, and there are a lot of reasons for that. It's not as simple as keeping products in a vault, because many burglaries happen at cultivation facilities, giant warehouses where licensees cultivate. The thieves come and steal pot plants. While we

What's Up with Delivery Services?

Before the passage of MMRSA and Prop. 64, the delivery of medical marijuana stood out as one of the grayest areas of a system already well known for its nebulous haze. Now delivery services are finally getting regulated by the state, but the majority of the rules affecting them will be hardly noticed by consumers or patients.

Really, the only significant change is the shift of power toward greater local control. Just a few years ago, it was unknown whether a city or county government had the power to ban medical marijuana deliveries within their jurisdictions. Since delivery cars move from place to face and are not fixed to any parcel of land, it appeared doubtful whether they could use their land use power to keep them out. And even if they could, no one knew conclusively whether such a rule would violate state constitutional protections forbidding local governments from meddling with commerce which happens to pass through their boundary lines.

MMRSA and Prop. 64 dispel all this delivery ambiguity with clear rules. Most significantly, they require delivery services to be licensed and subject them to veto power by any local government that wants to keep them from making drops in their town. This power even extends to cover delivery services which are based in a different county but drive an address within the regulating county to meet the customer. However, it is not unlimited: governments can regulate deliveries which are actually made within jurisdictions, and not delivery drivers who happen through to get to the next county.

opened the door to the industry, other cities closed their doors to large-scale cultivation, so we attract many cultivation facilities in Denver. What we did was restrict cultivation indoors. It is kind of a strange thing to be growing plants indoors but for many reasons, it actually makes sense to grow inside. However, now there are people who know how to target those facilities; maybe they worked as a trimmer previously and now have inside info, and we're seeing a variety of different tactics. One common approach is a stolen car driven through the warehouse door—then the thieves get as much as they can then take off in a different car. Not exactly sophisticated, but that's what we've seen. It's not a big number overall but it's a bit concerning that this specific type gets targeted as often as convenience stores or liquor stores.

So what we're doing is education. The industry is very sensitive about anything to do with violence within the industry. With the new federal attorney general there are concerns, (Jeff) Sessions is saying crime is up in Colorado —which is not true—and the industry wants help with this. The police department is willing to help and provide education but the industry doesn't want things misconstrued.

Q: *What about recent federal raids in Colorado (March 2017), what do those signify?*

A: The federal raids—that's something different, aimed to prevent diversion to the black market. There are organized syndicates coming here to "hide in plain sight." Ten years ago someone would have called in a warehouse that smelled like pot, but now you don't think twice about it. Both our amendments (medical marijuana in 2000, adult use legalization in 2012) allow you to grow for yourself and, in certain cases, for other people. What has been happening for some time is—people exploit that. "I'm a caregiver, this is for my cousin," they claim, and next thing we know we find these unlicensed warehouses with thousands of plants and no idea where the stuff is going. To combat that, the city passed a rule capping 36 plants for unlicensed grows in nonresidential settings. That has been successful in rooting out the warehouse grows but has forced them back to residential settings. We limit plants to 12 in any residential setting. Each adult gets 6, but in Denver it's capped at 12 plants per residence, no matter how many adults live there. There's a bill in the legislature to pass the rule statewide. We know that illegal home grows are serving the black market, including out of state. People on the East Coast will pay $6,000 per pound when locally it may be worth only $2,000. There have been several operations to take out some of the bigger grows. Those cases can take years to put together.

The two worlds, the licensed and unlicensed, are not always so separate. One of the raids was on a grow physically connected to a licensed business, and as an example in other cases you might see a warehouse divided into A, B, and C units. Units A and B were licensed, and unit C was black market. What's happened is that some people have come here to exploit the fact that it's accepted now. I think that this could be the result of Colorado being the first, and there are still millions of people who demand cannabis and can't access it legally. Who's supplying that? As long as there is a patchwork of states, there will always be a flow of products from where it can be grown well to where there's demand.

Q: *After these illicit grow moved back to residential neighborhoods, have you seen an increase in violent crime or burglaries in those neighborhoods?*

A: There have been a handful of altercations there, deals gone bad or burglaries. But mostly it's per se illegality, providing to the black market. We're concerned about this because we're going to protect our Denver quality of life. Denver is a great place to live. We're fine with legal marijuana, but don't mess with my quality of life. That's our goal as a policy team, to preserve that. If you supported legalization, great—you're happy as long as we're implementing it responsibly. If you didn't support it, we want to make sure that it won't affect your quality of life. Just as anything else, like the hash oil explosions we used to have, we have to be nimble and able to adjust our regulations quickly.

Q: *What has been the effect of legalization on road safety?*

A: Colorado Department of Transportation (CDOT) and the Colorado State Patrol (CSP) track those issues on a statewide level. Marijuana was never necessarily pulled out as a separate drug from alcohol or other drugs. We didn't track public consumption of marijuana until adult use legalization happened. Most of our statistics go back to 2013. But in Denver, we manually pulled all the crime data. In Denver specifically, there was an increase between 2013 and 2014, from 33 DUI-MJ incidents to 66 incidents. Compare to more than 2,500 total DUIs that year.

First of all, people have been driving around stoned in Denver for years. Colorado ranks near the top of national usage, and that has been true for years before we legalized. Until there are testing mechanisms in place that are as efficient or will stand up well in court as a breathalyzer, it's a harder thing to prove. The marijuana test is more time-consuming. Our focus is training our officers to get better at recognizing the signs. There are more people out there who can spot it, but we don't know if that will increase the number of arrests. But overall, CDoT has done a great job with their "Drive High, Get a DUI" campaign. Our overall DUIs have been dropping year after year, so that's good.

Q: *What about the concern that legalization will encourage more marijuana use by minors? Is Colorado "sending the wrong message" to teens?*

A: With teen use, we can't draw definitive conclusions any time soon. There are people on both sides who will argue passionately. See the Healthy Kids Colorado Survey, taken every two years. The last one that came out was the first one with data post-legalization. The good news is that usage rates did not increase significantly. They were already above the national average for 20 years but they did not increase further. What we have seen is a decrease in use perception of risk. That perception of risk could correlate with legalization, and there may be a lag between these perceptions and rates of use.

Q: *What about the legalization of medical marijuana? Have you seen more teens express lower perception of use risk because they think, "This is medicine, it can't be that bad?"*

A: We did not see the same effect for teens after medical legalization but that was not well publicized. After 2010 we saw the commercialization happen. But it was really recreational that put us on the map, because we were the first to do it. For weeks after the vote in 2012, and again after we opened stores in 2014, we saw ourselves on CNN all the time. This year we are doing a marketing and education campaign targeted at middle to high school students, providing resources for kids and adults who work with kids. There is a lot of interesting work being done. But unlike with cigarettes, there's a lot of young science.

CHAPTER TWO

The Law's Limits

ADULTS ONLY!

It's important to remember that while Prop. 64 is a legalization law that lifts many criminal prohibitions that used to apply to cannabis, it does not create a libertarian free-for-all in which people can suddenly do whatever they want with marijuana without legal consequences. In this section, I'll review what can still get you in trouble with the law, even after cannabis has been "legalized".

Prop. 64 makes cannabis use and possession legal only for adults over age 21. Not only do these provisions bring the regulation of cannabis use more in line with that of the familiar alcohol rules, they also mirror medical evidence showing that regular cannabis use tends to have a different effect on the developing brains of minors than on the more-developed brains of adults. So readers age 20 and under will have to wait, just as they do for buying alcohol and cigarettes.

The only real good news for California minors is that Prop. 64 significantly de-escalates the war against youth cannabis use, so that youthful indiscretions are discouraged without possibly ruining a young life before it begins. For example, a 17-year-old caught with a couple grams of hashish under the old laws could theoretically be subject to up to a year in jail. A youth of the same age and with the same amount will now be subject to mandatory drug education and community service. Possessing more than four grams of concentrate or over an ounce of marijuana, or bringing these products in any quantity onto school grounds while the school is open, subjects California minors to much more inconvenient education and service punishments. Dealers who specialize in high school hallways and lockers will feel that little has changed with the passage of Prop. 64.

Similar penalties apply to minors who are caught growing their own marijuana, even if they have their parents' permission. Adults over 18 but under 21 face possible fines.

California adults caught supplying marijuana to minors risk harsher penalties. Just possessing marijuana on school grounds can result in a hefty fine and up to 10 days in jail, even if they are not caught attempting to sell it. [11357(c)(2)]

Adults selling to minors, or employing minors in a marijuana business, can be charged with felonies and result in harsh penalties.

Whether it's a possession conviction that blocks a promising student from college or young children yanked away from desperate cannabis consumer parents, the most wrenching stories in the realm of cannabis policy usually have something to do with the relationship between children and parents. California's new cannabis laws bring some much needed clarity to this hazy and highly charged subject, but there are still some important pitfalls that every parent should be careful to avoid.

Don't share it with your kids! This may go without saying, but it is illegal for any California adult to share cannabis with any minor, regardless of whether they are members of the same family. The potential consequences of doing so are harsh: depending on the circumstances (and the age of the child), you could be charged with a felony and face multiple years in prison (not to mention the loss of your child to Child Protective Services)! Of course, there is a major exception to this rule, in the case of parents providing medicine to sick children who have a legal recommendation under MMRSA (see Patient FAQ).

Secure your stash. Although it is a less egregious offense than intentionally giving cannabis to your kids to ingest, allowing them to access your supplies through negligent inaction can also cause big problems. If you have custody of a child in California, you have extra responsibilities to keep them safe, and that includes keeping dangerous substances out of their reach. The principle is straightforward: if you wouldn't leave alcohol or prescription pills out where your curious kids can try putting them in their mouths, then you shouldn't do it for marijuana either.

This is no reason to panic if you're a patient worried about losing your kids: Prop. 64 specifies that medical marijuana patients will not be subject to state proceedings against their custody based on their status as patients alone. But while this is an important protection, it doesn't give you *carte blanche* to get as high as you want and ignore your kids' needs. You don't have to be perfect, and kids can be amazingly resourceful even in the face of the most fool-proof lock. But you will be expected to take all reasonable steps to make sure your enjoyment of your adult rights don't expose your children to any substance they shouldn't be getting into.

KEEP IT IN BOUNDS

Cannabis legalization is a terrific new freedom (or more precisely, a very old freedom that got briefly taken away and now is mostly restored), but it's only valid within California jurisdiction. This means that all of your legal protections to use and possess cannabis could effectively evaporate the moment you cross the boundary into another state or onto federal property.

This is a point that Prop. 64 makes quite clear, by underlining that adults who improperly either import or export cannabis for sale can be subject to harsh penalties—even a felony charge for repeated offenses [11360(b)-(c)]. In other words, you'll have to keep it in bounds—California cannabis must be grown in California, and it must stay in California from farm to ashtray. Anyone who attempts to subvert that rule takes a risk.

Holding marijuana in California can carry a bigger risk if you bring it from state to federal jurisdiction. The federal government still classifies marijuana as a Schedule I drug next to heroin. Cocaine, methamphetamine, and barbiturates have a lower classification, Schedule II, which allows them to be prescribed. Despite polls showing over 70 percent of Americans opposed to federal meddling in states that have passed marijuana reforms, the feds still reserve the right to meddle at will. (See "Will the Feds Trump State Law?," Chapter 3).

This means avoiding bringing marijuana onto any land under federal jurisdiction, including some of the best places on Earth to enjoy cannabis—California's national parks. While you may agree with me that any adult should be able to enjoy a joint overlooking Yosemite Valley so long as they don't litter or cause any fire risks, rangers enforcing federal law don't see things the same way. Until federal law finally changes, this is one privilege that will have to wait.

DRIVING

Driving under the influence of marijuana is generally not as dangerous as driving drunk, but the driving rules under

Prop. 64 fail to reflect this reality. Prop. 64 preserves the status quo. So let's take a look at what it says.

California Vehicle Code 23152(f) states: "It is unlawful for a person who is under the influence of any drug to drive a vehicle."

Sounds straightforward, but what does it actually mean? The California benchbook of jury instructions explains:

> "A person is under the influence of a drug when as a result of using a drug his/her physical or mental abilities are impaired to such a degree that he/she no longer has the ability to drive a vehicle with the caution characteristic of a sober person of ordinary prudence under the same or similar circumstances." [CALJIC 16.831]

If the judge or jury concludes that your driving failed to meet this "reasonable sober driver" standard, you can be punished. Generally a DUI is a misdemeanor in California, but it can be upgraded to a felony if you have enough of a prior record or if your drugged driving causes injury to someone else.. And if you get caught, don't think that your doctor's note will get you out of it: driving under the influence of cannabis in California is just as illegal, regardless of whether we're talking about recreational or medical use. Chronic pain patients don't get a free pass to get hopped up on steroids or opioids before getting behind the wheel, and neither do medical marijuana patients.

Prop. 64 also preserves prohibitions against open containers, which apply just as much to cannabis as they do to beer. Getting caught with an open bag or packed pipe in the car can net you a $250 fine on the first offense [11362.3].

One big advantage of choosing cannabis instead of alcohol is the far greater likelihood that you'll recognize when you've become impaired. Unlike drunk drivers, who all too often exaggerate their driving skills to themselves before provoking tragedy, stoned drivers are more likely to become paranoid about getting behind the wheel.

This is not to say that driving under the influence of cannabis is not a problem, but this difference between the judgments of drunk and stoned drivers may have had something to do with the ominous predictions of soaring fatal accident rates failing to materialize in legalizing states.

Roadside Drug Tests

Anticipating the wave of state legalizations, which has caught California and others in its wake, many states have invested in developing a marijuana sobriety field test, like the breathalyzer used by cops to test for blood alcohol content. So far, no technology has proved equally effective at detecting THC impairment (see "Ask a Cannabis Regulator," Chapter 1). Saliva, urine, and hair follicle tests can detect cannabis metabolites, which are the leftovers from the reaction that causes impairment.

They can detect prior marijuana use. Depending on the technology, they return a positive result even when the subject hasn't used marijuana in days or even weeks. Unlike alcohol, which is metabolized quickly by the body, cannabinoid metabolites linger for a long time. This creates testing problems, since a positive result for one of these tests does not necessarily indicate that the driver is under the influence.

Blood tests are more accurate, because they can detect active THC instead of just its leftovers. This technique does not eliminate all false positives, but it does a much better job since active THC remains in the blood for a few hours, not days. Fortunately, we have constitutional protections against cops forcing us to let them draw our blood based only on a hunch or suspicion of stoned driving or because the driver happens to fit a profile. The bottom line is, if you drive dangerously for any reason, including being impaired by marijuana, you can and probably should be pulled over.

For a more detailed discussion of marijuana testing technologies available to cops, see the *California NORML Guide to Drug Testing.*

CANNABIS IN THE WORKPLACE

Revenge of the Clerks?

I have some bad news for the eager hordes of disgruntled employees counting down the date to when they can finally blow triumphant billows of pot smoke in their boss's face.

Prop. 64 [11362.45] takes pains to emphasize that employers still have the right to set their own rules for conduct in their workplaces, including "smoke-free" and "drug-free" policies (even pharmacies are "drug-free workplaces").

This applies not only to "the use, consumption, possession, transfer, display, transportation, sale, or growth of marijuana in the workplace," but also the question of whether an employer can fire you because you tested positive for cannabis on a company drug test.

This is no trivial concern, because who can afford to live in California without a job? Depending on the method they use, your employer may choose to fire you for marijuana you used days or even weeks before the test; whether you used it responsibly off the clock will be irrelevant to the test results. All this begs an urgent question: can your employer fire you because you smoked cannabis at home, off the clock?

In California before the passage of Prop. 64 and MMRSA, the answer was a clear yes. In *Ross v. Ragingwire Telecommunications*, the California Supreme Court ruled that the Compassionate Use Act did not shield employees from being drug tested and fired for failing results even if they had a constitutional right under state law to use that drug. So before the passage of the state's new rules, the right to use medical marijuana in California has only been the right to be an unemployed patient.

Will the passage of adult use legalization reverse this policy? Events in Colorado have not been encouraging (see "Patient FAQ," Chapter 3). In a unanimous decision, Colorado's Supreme Court decided that employers have a right to set their own discriminatory policies regarding drug use off-hours. It didn't matter, the court ruled, that the substance Brandon Coats had been tested and fired for was now a legal one in the state; the continued illegality of cannabis on the federal level was enough to cover Dish Network's decision.

Unfortunately the broad language of Prop. 64, protecting the "ability of employers to have policies prohibiting the use of marijuana by employees and prospective employees," clearly favors any HR department that wants to drug test. And then there's the reality that many of the top employers in the state are interstate or even international corporations subject to federal jurisdiction; significantly both the California and Colorado decisions were based in part on the illegal status of cannabis under federal law. This thorny issue may plague legalization for years to come.

Flower of Attorney?

The other principal issue raised by Prop. 64 concerning marijuana in the workplace involves professional malpractice or negligence. Here, again, the law goes out of its way to make clear it changes nothing. If you're a lawyer in California and you show up to court noticeably high, you can expect disciplinary action. Prop. 64 doesn't change that. The same policy governs other professionals such as medical personnel, cops, air traffic controllers, and so on. In fact, there are so many ways to get fired for a positive drug test that for many Californians, their employers may have more say over their right to use a "legal" drug than their government does.

CALIFORNIA'S NEW RULES AT A GLANCE

PART 1—ADULT USE

Possession

▸ Adults may possess up to 1 ounce of marijuana and up to 8 grams of concentrate.

▸ Adults may share with other adults without compensation.

BUT:

▸ No one may share marijuana or concentrate with a minor (under 21).

▸ In drug-free zones (i.e., schools, day cares, playgrounds), you may not possess cannabis.

▸ Employer workplace policies are still enforceable.

▸ Inmates and parolees must still abide by the terms of their incarceration or parole.

▸ No open containers while driving on California roads.

Consumption

▸ Adults may consume cannabis on their private property or the private property of others with permission.

▸ Adults may consume cannabis at coffee shops or cafes if the place of business is licensed for on-site consumption.

▸ Smoking or vaping cannabis is unlawful anywhere smoking tobacco is forbidden.

▸ Rental agreements forbidding smoking in an apartment are enforceable.

▸ Driving under the influence of marijuana is still illegal.

Personal Cultivation

▸ Adults may grow up to 6 mature plants at a time for their personal use.

▸ Local governments may choose to raise, but not lower, this limit.

▸ Adults may keep the produce of their cultivation, above the 1 ounce possession limit, at home.

BUT:

▸ Local governments may reasonably regulate cultivation, up to and including requiring cultivation indoors or in a greenhouse.

▸ Tenants must have the permission of their landlords.

Transparency & Quality Control

▸ All cannabis products sold in California must be tested for potency and contaminants.

▸ Labels must reflect the results of this testing.

▸ Claims of regional appellation (i.e., "Mendocino Grown") or organic certification are now enforced by the state.

▸ Chain of custody is verified through a state-regulated "track and trace" system.

▸ By the time you read this the state will probably have already released even more new rules, so check for the latest updates at Edrosenthal.com

CALIFORNIA'S NEW RULES AT A GLANCE

PART 2—MEDICAL USE

Purchasing Limits

▸ Dispensaries may provide no more than 8 ounces of marijuana or 8 grams of concentrate to a single patient in a day.

BUT:

▸ The 8-ounce limit may be waived for a patient who has a doctor's recommendation specifying that they need more.

New Taxes

▸ Medical marijuana now taxed at a similar rate to adult use marijuana.

BUT:

▸ Indigent patients may apply for a waiver of local sales tax.

Child Custody

▸ Possession or cultivation of marijuana for medical purposes by parents is no longer grounds for action by Child Protective Services.

▸ Negligently leaving supplies of any drugs within the reach of young children could lead to problems with the state.

Cultivation

▸ MMRSA confirms and codifies the power of local governments to strictly regulate or even ban most medical marijuana cultivation within their jurisdictions.

BUT:

▸ Medical marijuana patients may still grow six plants pursuant to Prop. 64 (see facing page).

Ease of Obtaining Dr.'s Recommendation

▸ Doctors are now prohibited against writing clearly excessive recommendations.

▸ Doctors who write medical marijuana recommendations are now held to a minimum standard of patient care.

BUT:

▸ Most California doctors who write MMJ recommendations already comply with these rules.

▸ Other rules, such as a proposal to cap THC levels for edible medical marijuana doses, are pending at the state as of the time of this writing. Check Edrosenthal.com for the latest updates.

ASK:

Teen Use Experts—Rosalie Pacula, PhD, and Beau Kilmer, PhD

In a national debate characterized by shrill argument on all sides, very few voices offer what the RAND Corporation's Drug Policy Research Center has to say. Based in Oakland and led by Rosalie Pacula and Beau Kilmer, this group offers an honest and authoritative perspective on the various cannabis policy options on the menu for state governments and the likely effects of each choice. Strictly nonpartisan, RAND's only purpose is to better inform the debate.

Reading through the group's publication, "Considering Marijuana Legalization," it is immediately apparent why their work is so seldom weaponized as sound bites in the culture wars. Filled to the brim with caveats and epistemological limitations, the group's answer to nearly every question raised by legalization debates is some version of "It's complicated." But don't let this discourage you, because every page is well worth a read. In the interest of space, I have excerpted only sections pertaining to one of the most urgent questions surrounding Prop. 64—the possible effects of legalization on rates of teen abuse, not only of marijuana but of all drugs.

Q: *Perhaps the greatest concern about marijuana legalization is the potential effect on the brains of adolescents who may go on to use it. What does the evidence say?*

A: Volkow et al. (2014) reviewed the emerging body of evidence on possible adverse effects of marijuana on brain development. Although the studies on humans are strictly correlational, controlled experiments on animals suggest that a causal role for marijuana in these associations is plausible. But because several different factors influence brain development, the question remains: if marijuana changes brain development, does this lead to long-term negative consequences?

A recent neurological study comparing recreational users and nonusers found significant differences in gray-matter density in several brain regions involved in reward processing (Gilman et al., 2014), and these varied with frequency of use. As the authors recognize, these associations might not be caused by marijuana use and might even cause marijuana use, and their user and nonuser samples were matched only on a very limited set of variables. Still, the results are troubling, and longitudinal brain imaging studies might resolve some of the uncertainty.

Scientists and activists alike vigorously debate the claim that marijuana use produces cognitive impairment, much like earlier arguments about an amotivational syndrome. Even if one is convinced that there are acute effects, establishing that there are chronic, cumulative effects—possibly even irreversible effects—is much more challenging. Science is working hard to try to answer this question but cannot answer it definitively at this time.

Meta-analyses of the literature suggest that associations between marijuana use and cognitive functioning are fairly weak and somewhat inconsistent (Grant, Gonzalez et al., 2003; Schreiner and Dunn, 2012), and they appear to be limited to a subset of very heavy users who begin using very early.

Q: *What about education goals? Does marijuana use encourage teens to drop out of high school?*

A: The correlation between marijuana use and dropping out of high school is positive, but it is unclear whether the relationship can be attributable to cognitive effects, peer effects, both, or neither. Largely based on a series of longitudinal studies, the Hall (2014) review of the research concludes that "[r]egular adolescent cannabis users have lower educational attainment than nonusing peers"; however, his review raises important questions about how much of the relationship is causal. For example, the review highlights a recent Australian twin study that attributes the association to genetic and environmental factors instead of cannabis (Verweij et al., 2013) and suggests that this is consistent with two other US twin studies. The review also notes that "the adverse effects of cannabis use on educational outcomes may be amplified by school policies that exclude [that is, expel] students who are caught using cannabis from secondary school."

A recent article that combined samples from three longitudinal studies in Australia and New Zealand found that those who used marijuana daily before age 17 had significantly lower odds of completing high school and earning a college degree (Silins et al., 2014). Although the study found a statistically significant dose-response relationship, this is neither necessary nor sufficient for causation. The authors argue that the relationship between using marijuana and completing high school "probably does not arise from a reverse causal association," but they note that "this possibility remains plausible" (p. 291).

Another longitudinal study based in the United States by MacCaffrey et al. (2010) found that the apparent effect of marijuana use on dropping out of high school disappeared once they controlled for cigarette use. This led the authors to conclude that the effect of marijuana use on decisions to drop out was not attributable to a drop in cognition (because cigarette smoking does not seriously impair cognition). Additional analyses revealed that parental and peer influences could explain the marijuana-dropout relationship.

Q: *Assuming the worst-case scenario for this inconclusive data on the effects of teen marijuana use, and assuming that legalization would encourage more teen use (another question with no conclusive answer yet), would that necessarily make marijuana legalization bad for teens?*

A: Suppose that legalization led to a doubling of marijuana consumption of all sorts, including not only a doubling of controlled recreational use but also a doubling of compulsive abuse and dependence. One might well view this as a net bad because of all the marijuana-related harms discussed above.

However, the total social cost associated with alcohol abuse is very much larger than all costs and outcomes related directly to marijuana use. So if the doubling of marijuana use came about because all these new marijuana users switched from drinking alcohol, that could be a net win from a public health perspective, particularly if these people would have otherwise been binge drinking. Indeed, Caulkins, Hawken, Kilmer and Kleiman (2012) found that even a 10 percent reduction in alcohol abuse accompanying the doubling in marijuana use could be a net win for society.

Alas, that story of increased marijuana use being a substitute for alcohol use is not the only possibility. It is also possible for two consumer goods to be complements, such that, when market conditions change in ways that promote greater use (and abuse) of one, that might lead to greater—not lesser—use (and abuse) of the other. If marijuana and alcohol proved to be complements, and legalization led to any sizable increase in alcohol use and abuse, then legalization would be a net loss.

Nor is alcohol the only subject with which there could be important interactions. Suppose that legalizing marijuana caused even a 1 percent increase in tobacco smoking. Because tobacco kills well over 400,000 people in the United States every year; then, in that hypothetical, legalizing marijuana might—in the long run—cause 4,000 additional premature deaths per year, an outcome that could outweigh any plausible benefits of marijuana legalization.

For alcohol and for the other illegal drugs, the existing literature is ambiguous, with some studies pointing in one direction and others pointing in the opposite direction. For opioids, there is consistency [showing substitution effects], but perhaps only because there are so few studies. The one substance for which the literature provides clearer indication is the interaction with tobacco use, for which there is considerable evidence and it tilts strongly toward greater complementarity (i.e., greater marijuana use would be expected to lead to greater tobacco use).

CHAPTER THREE

A Time of Change

PATIENT STATUS

The Road Ahead for Patients

One of the biggest changes coming to California cannabis law does not come from Prop. 64—at least, not directly. MMRSA, the medical marijuana regulation law passed by the legislature in anticipation of adult use legalization, will transform the relationship between medical marijuana patients and their medicine. Prop. 64 includes some provisions to facilitate that change.

Prop. 64 takes pains at several points to limit its effects on California patients, but MMRSA is not so gentle. While it preserves the rights of Californians to access marijuana for medical purposes, MMRSA radically transforms the legal nature of how they can obtain it. And foremost on the chopping block is the collective system that has been the backbone of California cannabis for over a decade.

Instituted by the passage of SB 420 in 2003, the collective system powers nearly all of the distribution of medical marijuana in California today. On paper, the dispensaries and delivery services that provide Californians with their medicine are organized as collectives or cooperatives, sharing both resources and medicine with their member-patients. As long as they maintain not-for-profit operation and follow certain other rules, these dispensaries are able to use the "collective defense," which protects them from conviction of distributing cannabis.

On January 1, 2018, thanks to MMRSA, the collective defense will go away, almost 15 years after it went into effect. It will be replaced by a new system of regulated licenses, similar to Prop. 64's structure for adult use cannabis.

Patients won't have to sign up for membership when they visit a new dispensary, but the legal relationship they have had with their collective is being replaced by a more regulated system.

Your relationship with your doctor will also change. MMRSA attempts to end telemedicine and "pot docs" by requiring that the prescription writer be the patient's "attending physician" before recommending cannabis.

This doesn't necessarily mean that you have to go through your HMO and primary care physician to get an appointment to renew your recommendation. Under California law, "attending physician" is a term that sets minimum standards of what is expected of a doctor's care. Any good doctor should have little trouble meeting these requirements.

Prop. 64 extends patients greater protections for the confidentiality of their medical information [11362.713(a-d)]. The files of medical marijuana patients are extended the same protections as those of any other patient, so that gov-

New Proposed Medical Rules

As this book was going to press, the state announced a new set of first draft rules covering many different aspects of the operations of medical marijuana licensees under MMRSA. Most of these changes will only affect license holders "behind the scenes" and won't have any direct effect on patients, but some of them may exert a strong effect indeed on California consumers.

At the time this book went to press, these rules had not yet been finalized and are thus subject to change. But they do provide a useful glimpse at the kind of thinking the state has been using when considering how to regulate the medical marijuana industry which is about to be transformed by the state's new rules:

No late-night dispensaries? The new rules propose to limit the operating hours of dispensaries to between 6:00 am and 9:00 pm, Pacific time.

New purchase limits: The rules propose to limit the amount of medicine a dispensary may sell to a patient or caregiver in a single day, to 8 ounces of flower -- but this cap can be waived if the patient has a doctor's note specifying that they need more. The state has also proposed to limit the sale of concentrates to 8 grams per patient per day and to define a "dose" of edible medical marijuana as 10mg of THC and to limit the total THC in an edible package to 100mg.

No delivery by drone: Yes, they actually addressed this. The proposed rules go on to specify that medical marijuana deliveries must be made by a car with a GPS tracking system to an actual physical address—so no more back-alley deals to get your meds!

ernments can't simply snoop around in individuals' medical records.

Prop. 64 also provides for county-issued patient identification cards that reduce the sales tax of medical supplies. The cost of applying for the cards is capped at $100. Indigent patients can purchase the card at either half-price or, in some cases, receive it free.

Marijuana patients who are also parents are protected from Child Protective Services, which before the passage of Prop. 64, could take enforcement and custodial actions against fraught parents merely for using their medicine. Prop. 64 [11362.84] shields them against this threat by prohibiting state agencies from "restricting or abridging custodial or parental rights to minor children in any action or proceeding under the jurisdiction of family or juvenile court" or merely because the parent is acting in compliance with medical marijuana laws.

THE PRICE OF POT

Has the weed truly been freed if only the rich can afford it? In a country where over half its citizens now reside in a state with some kind of marijuana reform, the cost of cannabis, whether for medical purposes or just for kicks, has become one of the most urgent issues. Novice recreational users will find pot and a copy of *Dark Side of the Moon* a cheap fun evening compared to any night out at the bar, but for patients who need daily treatment, significant swings in the price of pot make major splashes in their treatment regimens.

Steve DeAngelo, the activist-turned entrepreneur who cofounded Oakland's Harborside Health Center (the largest marijuana dispensary in both California and the country) has repeatedly warned about impending increases in the price of medical marijuana under the three-tier distribution system by both MMRSA and Prop. 64.

Three-tier distribution prohibits marijuana sales directly from farmer to retailer or dispensary. Instead, a third party, a licensed distributor, buys the product from the farmer and then sells it to a dispensary or store. This is the same system in place for most of the alcohol sold in California, and true to the campaign's promise to "regulate marijuana like wine."

It's easy to see why Steve is concerned. Under the old system, Harborside could buy pounds directly from the farmers. When Harborside's buyer found a pound they liked, they could sign up the farmer for their collective then buy it directly. But under MMRSA and Prop. 64, Harborside will have to buy from middlemen instead, who will have their own licenses as well as their own costs to pay and profits to make. These increased costs will have to be paid by Harborside. This will force them to raise prices to their customers.

Prop. 64 and MMRSA impose new taxes on every stage of production. The farmer, retailer, and customer will all have their taxes to pay, and every layer will drive up the final price a little more. As a result, taxes will comprise a significant portion of the retail price.

Some authors predict that in spite of this, the price of pot will plummet with legalization. Caulkins, Hawken, Kilmer, and Kleiman in *Marijuana Legalization: What Everyone Needs to Know* (2012), write that in a fully legal environment, a single joint could cost about the same as a single ketchup packet.

So who's right? The PhDs, or the entrepreneur who's helped run a cannabis operation for over a decade?

Actually, they both have salient points. The experts, in their analysis, imagine an environment in which essentially all legal restrictions that could drive up the price of pot are removed. They don't account for the fine details of the kinds of regulations that have been put in place in states such as Colorado, Washington, and Oregon—and which are coming soon for California. In fact these regulations are designed, in part, to keep the price of cannabis from plummeting.

The ultimate price of buying legal marijuana under Prop. 64 will mostly depend on the choices made by the state. Sacramento could decide, for example, to restrict the number of licenses it issues to farmers or retailers; by restricting supply while demand remains constant, they could drive up the price. However, in a legally restricted or high tax market, the alternative market will take a larger share of consumer share. In fact the heaviest users of marijuana would have the most incentive to seek alternative sources, with lower tax-free prices.

Regulations also play a large role; while many of the rules for Prop. 64 license holders are contained in the law itself, other decisions have been postponed and left to the state to determine the fine details of how to apply the law. State regulators could choose to impose requirements that drive up the compliance costs of legal businesses, or they could allow businesses to find cheaper, more efficient, ways to comply with Prop. 64's rules and let competition lower the price. Essentially, Steve DeAngelo and the PhD experts agree on the same fundamental principle: the costs of growing the plant itself are small compared to the costs of dealing with the law.

This is the real danger of moving from a collective defense to a regulated system: the collective system is little regulated and that allows market forces to respond freely to customer demand. With little government power to restrict supply, growers and collectives can freely spread out to meet patient demand. This statewide process has driven marijuana prices down in recent years.

A regulated system based on licenses can offer some advantages, but if poorly implemented it can destroy price equilibrium.

Under MMRSA and Prop. 64, growers can only grow and sellers can only sell if they're licensed; that decision lies with the state. So if the government underestimates patient demand, they could issue too few licenses for too little marijuana, which would raise prices by restricting supply. Or they could get greedy for tax revenues and try to drive up prices deliberately, so they can tax every transaction more.

But the government would do well to remember that such tactics will only be self-defeating in the long run. As 40 years of California drug war history has shown, the whole market can easily go back underground at the first hint of hostile policy.

If Sacramento tries to restrict medical supplies, patients can go right back to the illicit market—defeating the whole policy experiment before it even has a chance to succeed. Indeed, some of this effect is probably inevitable, as there will be many California cannabis farmers who are unable to obtain a license and cannot risk going out of business just because the laws have changed. The city of Denver has already passed new rules limiting the size of gardens in an attempt to restrict its own homegrown underground grow scene (see "Ask a Cannabis Regulator," Chapter 1). Moves like these may restrict, but won't eliminate, the long-enduring illicit market, which will always remain easy enough to find for those who really need affordable medicine. No one knows for sure how this volatile mix will play out in the future price of cannabis.

Will the Feds Trump State Law?

Now that you understand all the new rules regulating the adult and medical use of cannabis in California, here comes the frustrating part: The federal government can undo the wishes of California voters. The US president still retains the legal right to dismantle it all with a few strokes of his pen.

The "supremacy clause" of the US Constitution holds that in any conflict between state law and federal law, the federal rule will be supreme. This is highly relevant for California, since both its medical law and its adult use legalization are in direct conflict with the federal Controlled Substances Act that lists cannabis as Schedule I and strictly forbids its cultivation and distribution. Thus, under federal law, California's consumers, patients, growers, retailers, and even regulating governments all make up one giant organized crime ring.

The reality on the ground is not quite so simple. Although federal law is supreme to California's cannabis laws, there remains the separate question of whether the feds can actually enforce their policy. This question is complicated by the fact that Congress has repeatedly passed the so-called CJS amendment to its regular spending bills. This is also known as the Rohrabacher-Farr amendment after the two Congressmen who originally sponsored it (Dana Rohrabacher is a Republican representing Orange County). Rohrabacher-Farr declares that no money in the federal budget will be available to inhibit states from implementing their medical marijuana laws; that means the Department of Justice won't even have the money to buy the paper that its cease and desist letters would otherwise be printed on.

Some medical marijuana advocacy organizations argued for a broad interpretation of this amendment that would forbid federal prosecutors from targeting either state governments or the growers and distributors they regulate.

Others disagree with this, in favor of a much narrower interpretation that applies to state bureaucracies only. So far, federal judges have been split in their decisions as to which interpretation of this amendment is correct, so it's far from clear whether the US government retains the power to shut dispensaries down. And in any case, the CJS amendment must be renewed every year, and it's anyone's guess how much longer Congress may decide to do so.

There is an even murkier question of what, exactly, President Trump intends to do about California and other states' marijuana laws. On the campaign trail, Trump declared that the issue of medical marijuana should be left to the states, though he expressed skepticism about adult use legalization. Yet this middle-of-the-road declaration was belied by his later actions as President, such as nominating known hard-liners like Jeff Sessions into positions of power over drug policy. His inconsistent speeches and actions have made it particularly difficult to know what he may do.

In the end, the only real check on federal power against shutting legalization down is the voice of the American people. Polls show that many voters who do not necessarily support legal marijuana remain opposed to the federal government interfering with state policies.

Practical considerations dictate that the DEA and other federal agencies need the cooperation of state governments to enforce cannabis law. The feds don't have enough cops to enforce federal law in states that have chosen to legalize. Changing the situation would require such massive tax hikes and such an intrusive federal presence that attempting to go it alone risks a massive backlash. The DEA can make itself a big nuisance, but it cannot reasonably shut legalization down. Until Californians themselves decide to change them, California's new rules for marijuana are here to stay.

Double Standards

PROFILING.

For many readers, the topic is one they've read about occasionally, or perhaps not at all. Maybe it's a matter of social conscience, an issue for which they may try to raise awareness through social media or sharing articles online.

But if you're young, male, and not white in California, there's a good chance that police harassment is a regular part of your life. In 2012, the ACLU found that racially disparate enforcement was a national problem, prevalent in all 50 states; and for all its progressive attitudes, California is no exception.

I know about this effect, from the other side of the racial divide. In 2015, Berkeley police arrested me for growing cannabis in my backyard. I had a medical right to grow it, but my garden was technically in violation because I had failed to post all of the required paperwork.

But—nothing happened. After locating my doctor's recommendation, the cops let me go; they didn't even bother to write up an arrest report, so I can't even say that I became a statistic. My white skin was a highly effective defense.

But the ACLU report shows that African Americans living in the Golden State are more than twice as likely to be arrested for cannabis crimes than whites, despite the fact that white and black Californians use the drug at similar rates. Profiling is the biggest reason for this disparate effect: when cops observe a young black man doing something exactly the same as his white counterparts, they are more likely to see him as a criminal.

Prop. 64 recognizes this injustice and takes steps to correct it. First and most importantly, for California teens of every race, it replaces the heavy hand of the criminal law with the more helpful and effective tools of drug education and community service. While making firmly clear to teens that the use or sale of marijuana is an activity reserved for adults, Prop. 64 prefers penalties that won't burden them years into the future. Subsequently, petty cannabis offenses committed by students will be sealed on their 18th birthday, and offenses committed by teens 16 to 18 years old will remain on their record only two years.

Prop. 64's second strategy is to provide a path for adults with cannabis convictions to clear their records, and for adults currently serving penalties for cannabis offenses to petition to have their sentences commuted or reduced. If this section applies to you, look for an attorney who can help you expunge your record in appendix B at the back of this book.

Finally, Prop. 64 earmarks a portion of the tax revenue collected by the state to reinvest in the California communities most devastated by the legacy of many decades of drug war policy. It is hoped that this three-pronged approach will begin to reverse one of the worst aspects of the prohibition of cannabis in California: its cruel treatment of the state's most vulnerable communities.

Patient FAQ Section

BEFORE THE PASSAGE OF PROP. 64, ALL LEGAL CANNABIS use in California was medical. Now with adult use legalization underway, big changes are coming to the way the state regulates medical marijuana. The biggest changes will happen behind the scenes in the way the state regulates dispensaries and commercial growers, and some of these changes will affect patients, either directly or indirectly. Here are some of the top questions California patients have about the coming changes:

Q: *Will MMRSA reverse the medical marijuana ban passed by my city or county?*

A: No; if anything, MMRSA's implementation may further restrict medical marijuana access at the local level, though it mainly just cements the status quo. Ironically, the saving grace for many patients may be their right to grow six plants for adult use under Prop. 64.

One of the principal changes MMRSA makes to California's dispensary system is to impose a licensing system that controls all but the smallest medical gardens and all distributors. One of the new rules concerning these licenses requires that a licensee be approved at both the state and local level. Cities and counties will have effective veto power over whether to allow dispensaries within their jurisdictions—a power they already enjoy, thanks to a series of California Supreme Court decisions that opened the floodgates to a wave of bans up and down the state (see appendix A).

So on this issue, MMRSA mainly just codifies what the courts have already declared, except in the case of delivery services.

Q: *What makes delivery services different?*

A: Under the old rules, medical marijuana delivery services operated in one of the many gray areas of California cannabis law. Local governments had the power to regulate medical marijuana collectives within their jurisdictions but the California Constitution also puts certain limits on cities and counties trying to block organizations coming from outside to do business there. It was never conclusively resolved whether this meant that a county could, for example, ban a delivery service with an office just on the other side of the county line from coming over and making drops.

MMRSA closes this loophole by declaring that "deliveries, as defined in this chapter, can only be made by a dispensary and in a city, county, or city and county that does not explicitly prohibit it by local ordinance." This means that the delivery services of today will need to either obtain a license or close down, and it also means that cities will have a clearly defined power to ban deliveries as well as brick and mortar dispensaries. But the same section also provides that "[a] local jurisdiction shall not prevent carriage of medical cannabis or medical cannabis products on public roads by a licensee acting in compliance with this chapter," so this local authority only resides within the city or county where the medicine will actually be delivered; a licensed delivery service won't have to seek separate permission from every city and county they happen to cross before meeting the patient to make the delivery.

Q: *Will I be able to stay a member of my favorite collective?*

A: In effect, yes—but only if your collective is able to obtain a license.

The effect of MMRSA on the state's former collective system is nicely summed up in the legislative analysis of AB 266, one of the three bills that combine to make MMRSA:

"Under existing law, certain persons with identification cards, who associate within the state in order collectively or cooperatively to cultivate marijuana for medical purposes, are not solely on the basis of that fact subject to specified state criminal sanctions. This bill would repeal these provisions upon the issuance of licenses by licensing authorities pursuant to the Medical Marijuana Regulation and Safety Act, as specified, and would instead provide that actions of licensees with the relevant local permits, in accordance with the act and applicable local ordinances, are not offenses subject to arrest, prosecution, or other sanction under state law."

So, technically, the collective system is going away. But for the members of those collectives that successfully navigate the process of obtaining a medical marijuana license, there won't be many apparent differences. In fact, except for new rules requiring greater transparency on the labels of medical marijuana products, the only likely difference for patients will be an increase in price (see "The Price of Pot," Chapter 3).

Q: *Will I be able to keep my MMJ doctor?*

A: Probably so. SB 643, another of the bills comprising MMRSA, brings some regulation to the relationship between medical marijuana patients and their doctors, but really all it does is legislatively require the kinds of best practices that the majority of pot docs are already practicing anyway.

MMRSA does ask the state medical board to investigate "repeated acts of clearly excessive recommending of cannabis to patients for medical purposes, or repeated acts of recommending cannabis to patients for medical purposes without a good faith prior examination of the patient and a medical reason for the recommendation" (Sec. 220.05). In reality the law is not that extreme. Any good California doctor should have little trouble complying with this provision, regardless of whether the majority of their business is medical marijuana recommendations or something else.

Similarly, MMRSA forbids doctors to "recommend medical cannabis to a patient, unless that person is the patient's attending physician, as defined by subdivision (a) of Section 11362.7 of the Health and Safety Code." But this definition of "attending physician" is not that strict either.

Any doctor who physically examines the patient and performs a good faith diagnosis can comply with this rule as well, so in practice all it really forbids is "telemedicine," a euphemism for doctors writing MMJ recommendations over Skype. While the final rules have yet to be announced, at this point it's safe to predict that the state will require medical marijuana recommendations come from doctors who first physically examined the patient, in the same room.

Q: Can I keep my relationship with my caregiver?

A: Probably so, but MMRSA takes steps to provide clear rules restricting the size of caregiver operations, so that de facto commercial operations can't try to pass themselves off as caregivers, similar to what happened in Denver after commercial medical marijuana legalization there in 2010 (see "Ask a Cannabis Regulator," Chapter 1). If your provider is a true caregiver, operating in the same spirit of the law authorized by the Compassionate Use Act in 1996, this rule will probably not affect them. By restricting caregivers to small, nonprofit operations for the benefit of no more than five patients, MMRSA aims to restore the kind of personal, compassionate attention that was the original foundation of California's medical marijuana laws.

As already discussed, MMRSA generally requires all MMJ providers to be licensed, but this rule "does not apply to a primary caregiver cultivating marijuana pursuant to Section 11362.5 if the area he or she uses to cultivate marijuana does not exceed 500 square feet and he or she cultivates marijuana exclusively for the personal medical use of no more than five specified qualified patients for whom he or she is the primary caregiver within the meaning of Section 11362.7 and does not receive remuneration for these activities, except for compensation provided in full compliance with subdivision (c) of Section 11362.765."

Q: *Can I keep my medical marijuana garden?*

A: Yes, but that depends on your garden's size and location, and whether you need the permission of your landlord. Adults who own their own property can grow at least six plants for their own use, and this product can be used for medical purposes if they need to do so.

In general, MMRSA requires all medical gardens to be licensed—a time-consuming and expensive process that most individual patients won't be able to afford. But the law also provides an exception to this rule for "a qualified patient cultivating marijuana pursuant to Section 11362.5 if the area he or she uses to cultivate marijuana does not exceed 100 square feet and he or she cultivates marijuana for his or her personal medical use and does not sell, distribute, donate, or provide marijuana to any other person or entity."

One hundred square feet isn't much. I've seen some individual plants in Mendocino County that take up almost that much area all by themselves! While the requirement that patient gardens be only for personal use is a reasonable one, the small size permitted by this rule could become a big issue for the state's sickest patients.

Yet for many local governments in California, even a 10 ft. by 10 ft. square is too much cannabis garden to countenance, which is why MMRSA further clarifies that "[e]xemption from the requirements of this section does not limit or prevent a city, county, or city and county from regulating or banning the cultivation, storage, manufacture, transport, provision, or other activity by the exempt person, or impair the enforcement of that regulation or ban." So under MMRSA, your local government has the power to restrict that 100 square feet down to zero—but as a practical matter, this provision changes little. Any government likely to exercise this provision will have probably already banned cannabis gardens anyway.

Q: *Will the price of medical marijuana change?*

A: Good question. See "The Price of Pot," Chapter 3.

Q: *Will MMRSA make medical marijuana safer to use?*

A: Yes. Most of the state's medical marijuana supplies are already safe to use due to industry self-regulation, but MMRSA's rules are designed to make sure that 100 percent of Californian medical cannabis meets strict standards.

It has become customary for California dispensaries to require laboratory testing of their products in response to consumer demand; given the choice, most patients prefer to pay a little extra for cannabis that they can be sure is free of pesticides, mold, and other contaminants. But despite this, not all medical marijuana dispensed in California is lab-tested. Further, while all California cannabis labs test for the presence of chemical adulterants, there is yet no consensus on which treatments, including "organic" treatments, are safe to apply to plants destined for sick patients.

Under MMRSA, this situation is about to change. Once it fully takes effect, it will require all medical cannabis supplies to be tested by licensed laboratories, according to standards developed by the Department of Pesticide Regulation and the Department of Food and Agriculture out of Sacramento. These departments are empowered by the law to convene advisory boards including patient and industry representatives, but they are not required to do so.

Because self-regulation is already common, these rules will not necessarily set off a revolution in medical cannabis safety; but if they work as designed they will still make an important difference for California patients.

Q: *Will labels on medical marijuana products become more transparent?*

A: Yes and no. Most medical marijuana labels in California today already provide useful information for consumers due to competition and industry self-regulation, but few products distributed under the old system meet the same level of exacting transparency as will soon be required by MMRSA.

Today, patients frequenting any of California's cannabis dispensaries usually find information on the tested potency of their medicine, including THC and CBD. Some provide information about other cannabinoids, usually CBN and CBG, and some post information regarding the most common terpenes such as caryaphelene, limonene, and myrcene.

MMRSA'S
NEW REQUIREMENTS

▸ But MMRSA requires posting levels of a broader list, adding THCa, CBDa, CBG, CBN, and the most common terpenes. These are plant odor chemicals that give cannabis its smells and also enhance the action of cannabinoids. The state can also expand the list to "any other compounds required by the State Department of Public Health."

▸ Every label must also contain a statement of whether the cannabis product exceeds permitted levels of contaminants, a broadly defined term that includes everything from chemical residues to microbes to dust, cat hair, and dander.

▸ MMRSA also sets organic standards for California cannabis. Many of the state's growers already sell "organic" cannabis, but before MMRSA there was no consensus about exactly what that meant.

- MMRSA-regulated labels will include regional appellations enforced by the state, so consumers will know with confidence from which region (such as Mendocino County or the Sierra foothills) their medicine came.

- Finally, MMRSA-regulated labels will also include state-mandated warnings to keep supplies out of the reach of children, and a helpful reminder that the federal government still considers cannabis a Schedule I substance with no medical value, a designation that flies in the face of all available evidence.

Q: *Will my medical information be private under MMRSA?*

A: Yes. MMRSA allows state agencies to divulge only the minimum amount of information necessary to verify that a marijuana consumer is a legitimate patient, and no more. In every other regard, a medical marijuana patient's medical records are accorded the same privacy protections as all other California patients.

Q: *If my medical use is legal and regulated, can my employer still fire me for failing a drug test?*

A: This question has not been fully resolved. MMRSA clarifies that its provisions "shall not interfere with an employer's rights and obligations to maintain a drug and alcohol free workplace or require an employer to permit or accommodate the use, consumption, possession, transfer, display, transportation, sale, or growth of cannabis in the workplace or affect the ability of employers to have policies prohibiting the use of cannabis by employees and prospective employees, or prevent employers from complying with state or federal law."

This rule would seem to clearly empower employers to forbid their employees from using marijuana at work, even for medical reasons; but what is far less clear is whether they could legally fire employees for medical marijuana use at home and off the clock. The clause protecting "the ability of employers to have policies prohibiting the use of cannabis by employees and prospective employees" would seem to protect any employer that wants to fire a worker for failing a drug test; but at the same time, under the Compassionate Use Act, Californians have a constitutional immunity against certain consequences of their medical marijuana use.

Decisions on these issues will be up to the courts, but recent cases in California and out of Colorado may be an omen. (See "Cannabis in the Workplace," Chapter 2).

Q: *Can my landlord forbid me from using medical marijuana in my apartment?*

A: Not entirely, but landlords may place certain restrictions on how tenants consume cannabis on their premises. Prop. 64 preserves the right of landlords to set rules on their property, and this would seem to include smoking cannabis [sec. 11362.45(h)]. It is unclear whether a patient's right to possess medical marijuana, as a right enshrined in the state constitution, would trump a landlord's right to maintain a smoke-free home—yet another of the many questions that will have to be worked out in the years to come.

But one area where patients seem to be on solid ground is edibles, tinctures, vaporizers, and any other means of taking their medicine that doesn't involve smoke. Landlords may complain about this; but it's hard to see how they would be in any way harmed by it.

Q: *Does the 21 year-old age limit for recreational cannabis under Prop. 64 apply also to medical marijuana patients?*

A: No—but that doesn't mean you can simply go cut gym class and get your weed card (sorry). California doctors are legally allowed to recommend medical marijuana to patients of any age according to their professional judgment, but there are very good reasons why a doctor may hesitate to recommend marijuana to an underage patient. One good reason is that the side effects of regular medical marijuana use are much more severe for youth than for adults (see "Ask Teen Use Experts," above). Another good reason is that a practice of handing out MMJ recommendations to any high school student who requests one is a sure-fire way to run a doctor afoul of MMRSA's prohibitions against "clearly excessive recommendations" (see above) and thus lose their professional license. The laws are written to enable child patients who actually need medical marijuana to access it but to discourage access for all other minors.

Q: *Will the state limit how much medical marijuana I can purchase at a time?*

A: It's not a sure thing yet, but as of the time this book was going to press the state bureaucracy was hard at work creating a framework to do just that. Included in the first draft of MMRSA's proposed rules are proposals to:

Limit the amount of cannabis a dispensary may sell to a patient in a day to 8 ounces (but this limit can be waived if the patient has a doctor's note specifying that they need more).

Limit the amount of concentrate a dispensary may sell to a patient in a day to 8 grams.

Limit packages of medical marijuana edibles to 10 "doses" of 10mg each.

As of this writing these rules had not been finalized but they probably would be soon enough.

Ask a Patient

FOR ANGELA BACCA, WHO WAS DIAGNOSED WITH Crohn's disease just before starting her freshman year at San Francisco, medical marijuana has been a tremendous help. It has not cured her debilitating and painful disease, but using it has allowed her to substantially reduce her reliance on surgeries and powerful pharmaceutical steroids. Cannabis medicines have allowed her to live a near normal life. As a medical marijuana patient who grew up in California but has also lived in Oregon and Utah, she brings a unique perspective to the question of how marijuana policy can affect patients, for either better or worse.

Q: *Describe a bad day in the life of a Crohn's disease patient.*

A: A bad day starts out with me waking up starving and nauseated. I dry-heave over the toilet for a while, then I'll smoke cannabis to take care of the nausea, then I decide whether I want to eat and brace myself for the pain that makes me feel like my colon is going to explode inside of me. It is frustrating because I have struggled to pay medical bills and maintain coverage my entire life, yet my doctors can't actually help me improve my quality of life. They can only prescribe drugs. It is frustrating to have to teach yourself how to treat yourself while you are suffering and paying someone else everything you earn to stay alive.

Q: *As a medical patient you lived in Utah, which has a very limited MMJ law; California, which has a liberal MMJ law; and Oregon, which has both an MMJ law and adult use legalization. From your personal experience, which system affords the best access for you as a patient? Comparing California and Oregon in particular, does the addition of adult use legalization expand or restrict your access?*

A: The best system for access for me was the one that existed before MMRSA. I had a caregiver and all supplies were affordable. Here in Oregon I am rationing my oil because my oil provider doesn't have the license to continue producing it for the medical market without interruption. Ninety-five percent of the market in Oregon is now categorized as recreational. The caregiver program is almost done because it's hard to find caregivers. When Oregon split the system, they disincentivized medical production.

In October, when full recreational sales and regulations took effect, there was a bottleneck in approving state-licensed labs, and those still performing them increased their prices by 400 percent. There were very few products legally available anywhere for months and the prices were very high. It is still difficult to find extracts and manufactured products, but it is getting a bit easier. And servings of the oil are capped at 100 mg.

They promised us that the medical system would not change. That was not true. Why do the medical and recreational supplies need to be separate? How about letting the growers grow for both markets? Despite the classification the government prescribes to the user, they are using the same things and growing the same way. The products aren't different, just the reasons for use. I think that splitting the market was meant to incentivize pharmaceutical cannabis development and to push more botanical use into the highly taxed "recreational" classification. [Author's note: Unlike in Oregon, under Prop. 64 and MMRSA, both kinds of cannabis are taxed at similar rates.]

Q: *MMRSA requires all MMJ recommendations to come from the patient's attending physician, which essentially prohibits telemedicine, and aims to restrict "excessive" recommendations by doctors. As a patient, are you concerned about these regulations, or are you rather encouraged by the law's attempts to rein in perceived excesses?*

A: I completely understand that. I've been to plenty of events where there's the line to see the MMJ doctor next to the ATM before you get into the medical area. This is clearly making a mockery of medicine to do it this way; but in their defense, these doctors also know that cannabis is safe to use and not to possess, so I don't disagree with them manipulating the law to both make money (which is the point of being a doctor in this country) or to legally protect people who want to use cannabis but don't have a serious medical diagnosis. If a healthy person chooses cannabis over aspirin for a headache, it's a positive medical choice. If a healthy person chooses to unwind after a long day with a joint instead of a beer, that is a positive medical choice. I don't disagree with doctors or users manipulating the law to ensure their freedom and grant them safe access.

I am no longer worried about recreational users misrepresenting the real medical patients like myself because I think the general public, at least in the United States, has come to a consensus about the medical use of marijuana. Vast majorities of Americans support it for medical uses now. I have never, at least not in recent memory, had anyone doubt the legitimacy of cannabis to treat my Crohn's symptoms, even if they were opposed to legalization. These recreational users were important to the medical market though, because they subsidized it for people like me who need it to function.

Q: *What is your opinion of rules in MMRSA and Prop. 64 mandating laboratory testing, creating standards for organic practices and regional appellations, and imposing minimum labeling requirements? Have similar rules in Oregon benefited you as a patient, compared to the previously lightly regulated MMJ industry of California?*

A: It does help me make decisions, and that's the best way to choose a treatment. I'm glad to see standardization of pesticide testing, since a pesticide can slip through if it's not tested for.

But I don't think California's medical industry was lightly regulated; I think it was largely self-regulated. Look at Harborside, which tried to create a competitive advantage by labeling their products with lab tests. They helped found Steep Hill Laboratory to do it. Patients started reporting back that higher CBD products were creating specific positive effects for them, then the information traveled back up through the budtender to the buyer to the grower to the breeders, who in turn bred CBD back up. This is how we discovered what CBD can do, years before Sanjay Gupta publicized it. It would not have been possible without the hundreds of thousands of small farms that supply the West Coast cannabis market. If state laws move toward mega-grows and vertical licensing, and sets significant barriers to entry into the legal market to small producers, we will lose the sort of genetic diversity that leads to discoveries of the magnitude of the medical benefits of CBD.

Q: *Concerning quality control, has the lack of transparency ever negatively affected you as a patient?*

A: In Utah, Fourth of July 2014, I had been in a lot of pain but I wanted to get out and see my friends. I ran out of joints halfway through. I had to buy some cannabis locally. I went to Rose Park, and I paid $150 for a half ounce. I smoked it and I got nauseous and everyone else did too. This is what happens in Utah or Kansas or Oklahoma, they end up smoking the unhealthy bud that can't be sold in

California. This is the need for a national standard. Am I any less sick on the Utah side of the border?

Q: *MMRSA and Prop. 64 essentially codify rules that have been developed by judges granting wide latitude to local governments to regulate or even ban MMJ activity in their jurisdictions. Prop. 64 does carve out a six-plant exception statewide for those who can comply with the regulations. How much hardship would you face having to travel to another county to get the supplies you need?*

A: That's a problem here in Oregon too. Is it fair that just because some people don't want to see a pot shop, I don't get to treat myself? The patchwork of local regulations is part of the problem for us patients. You don't want to look at or smell it? Well guess what—I don't want to suffer.

My parents live in a rural, conservative part of California that has instituted such a ban. When I go down to visit them, the closest brick and mortar dispensary is two hours away. So I have to stock up in San Francisco or Los Angeles before visiting them.

Q: *MMJ is not covered by insurance. Steve DeAngelo has warned that the three-tier distribution system created by MMRSA and Prop. 64 will inevitably increase the price of cannabis for consumers, and that the new laws impose high taxes on both medical and adult use supplies. Oregon does not mandate three-tier distribution, and while its taxes on adult use supplies are high, its taxes on medical supplies are low. As a patient, do you notice a big difference between the price of medical marijuana and adult use marijuana in Oregon? What are the prices like? Are they affordable for you?*

A: What's happened in Oregon in October 2015 is—there were so many growers here that the price of an ounce was under $100 after legalization. There were about 300 dispensaries in Portland, all licensed, all medical. Once recreational legalization set up, licensing was too slow and convoluted, and many growers couldn't deal with it. The prices have skyrocketed because of the testing bottleneck, which led to the new, higher testing prices, and the fact that a lot of growers can't afford to, or manage to, stay in the legal market.

I am lucky to still have a caregiver, but the way the state set it up, that will be gone soon, too. With an almost nonexistent medical market there really isn't a reason for growers to try to produce for it. I still have my caregiver, so I am lucky. I get an ounce of flower and 15 grams of oil a month from Oregon caregivers. The cost of that medicine at retail would be between $500 and $1,000 a month. In addition to that base of FECO and flower, I buy less than $100 a month worth of dabs, since neither of my caregivers give me that. Right now I spend $100 a month and receive about $700 a month in-kind.

Now it costs $30 to $40 for 1 gram of FECO oil, and high-CBD wax costs $90 to $100 per gram. Many patients need that much per day to treat their conditions. This is happening because there's a push now to say these products are not medicine, as compared with pharmaceutically produced Sativex and Epidiolex. That policy is great for business, not for patients.

It's empowering to be able to provide my own medicine, to take care of myself, and to be responsible for treating my own symptoms with a plant I grew myself. It is liberating to not be anxiously tied to the pharmaceutical-industrial complex for the rest of my life.

ASK:
A Drug War POW—Dr. Lakisha Jenkins

After a decisive vote for legalization, it is tempting to speak of the drug war, and all the ugliness that attended it, as a bygone chapter of history. But while Prop. 64 drastically reduces or eliminates cannabis penalties across the board, the heavy hand of the criminal law is not entirely stayed, and mere possession of one ounce of marijuana and one gram of concentrate by an adult age 18 or over can still trigger a misdemeanor charge. Any remnant of the drug war means that the uncomfortable questions of how the criminal laws are used, and against whom, must also remain part of the discussion.

Lakisha, a naturopathic doctor and herbalist based in Merced, opened her own nonprofit medical marijuana and herbalism clinic after the death of her young daughter from the side effects of the chemotherapy her doctors prescribed to treat her brain cancer. Lakisha's clinic treats cancer patients at low cost or even free of charge, and integrates medical marijuana into a full herbal pharmacopeia—a model that has garnered her plenty of attention, both positive and negative. While her innovative clinic earned her a seat as the president of the California Cannabis Industry Association (CCIA), it also attracted the notice of local police, who have arrested and raided her multiple times. As of the time of this writing, Dr. Jenkins has not been convicted of any crime and still has yet to see the evidence against her. We will hear from her what it is like to become the target of aggressive law enforcement, despite her good faith belief in her compliance with the state's medical marijuana laws.

Lakisha went from being one of California's top cannabis entrepreneurs to a sobering reminder that the drug war is still not over, even after legalization. As a mother, as a naturopathic doctor and licensed herbalist, and as an industry leader, she can speak knowledgeably about both the benefits and potential harms of cannabis; but now as a target of sustained persecution by the local police where she lives and works, she can speak just as knowledgeably about what it is like to be on the wrong side of the law.

After multiple arrests, a raid on her clinic garden, and over a year of court battles, Lakisha has not been convicted of any crime. In fact, on two separate occasions, local police arrested her and confiscated "evidence" from her philanthropic activities without charging her with any violations at all. I asked her about her work as a naturopath and patient advocate, as well as her experience of being targeted by cops for distributing a substance that California voters demanded be legalized for over 20 years.

Q: *First, can you describe the medical marijuana collective model you developed in Merced, how it was* *born, and how it is different from other state collectives?*

A: We built a 501(c)(3) holistic health charity mostly focused on cancer survivors. Through it, we provide direct financial assistance: we help pay for food, rent, utilities, whatever it takes to get them through treatment. I don't believe that it's fair for someone who's facing a life threatening disease to have to make life-altering decisions on a daily basis.

The Kiona Foundation is really the heart and soul of our business. My oldest daughter, Kiona, was diagnosed with brain cancer when she was eight years old. At the time, I didn't want for anything. I was doing well for myself—and my family. But a cancer diagnosis changes that because we started having to pay expenses out of pocket. It got so bad I called the American Cancer Society (ACS). We had done Relay for Life and raised $15,000 for them. And then I asked the Cancer society for $238 for car payment because of all the trips to Sacramento——and co-pays were outrageous. But they told me that they are a research organization and don't really offer financial assistance. They offered a $200 per year mileage reimbursement, and assistance finding a carpool in case I lost my car.

As a naturopathic doctor, I can certainly understand the need for more cancer research. But they're a foundation that pulls in over $850 million in revenue a year. Their CEO is paid an annual salary of $863,000. Our Relay for Life team *alone* raised $15,000 the year prior, and the one thing we need help with, we couldn't get. That's how the Kiona Foundation was born—there needed to be a charity to help families who are facing hard choices: do we eat this month or do we make the car payment?

So we started Kiona Foundation in 2003, the year after the diagnosis. We provided direct financial assistance to cancer survivors as a charity. And after we opened, the ACS started referring people to us! We have nowhere near their budgets, but we're the ones who provided the assistance.

After a while I realized the foundation wasn't as effective as it could be. There were new cancer diagnoses cropping up in California at a terrifying rate, and we didn't have enough money to help them all. That was not OK with me. So we switched gears and became a holistic health organization—one focused to help you learn how not to get cancer in the first place. So let me help you learn how not to get cancer; or if you do, there are herbs which can help save your life or help you have a better quality of life. Unlike other medical collectives, we don't treat cannabis as our only product. At my office, it's just one of many herbs that I, as a licensed herbalist, may consider offering to a patient.

Kiona passed away in 2006, even though the doctors successfully removed her tumor on her second surgery. But she could not recover from the chemo and radiation, and that's what killed her. She technically beat brain cancer, but the treatment killed her? That's not OK! That's where this model was born—out of patient advocacy, to educate people that there are alternatives. There are ways to complement these dangerous treatments or forgo them entirely.

Q: *After starting this foundation, you became the president of the California Cannabis Industry Association. What was your focus in that role?*

A: I am and have been a patient advocate. This industry was built by patients fighting for their lives and by caregivers trying to help them. We need to not go down the road of Washington State, where the medical system was wiped out. Eight grams does not cover the amount that a cancer survivor needs. You can't legislatively bar patients from having access just because that could jeopardize the adult use supplies.

Before I became CCIA president, I felt that my concerns about patient rights and restorative rights weren't being honored. Prop. 64 didn't have any provisions for restorative rights until I started raising hell about it. Then they got the NAACP on board and they got some provisions in. It was me and Steve DeAngelo who were the primary voices on that, initially. If it weren't for the industry leaders talking about these things, it would not have happened. And no, I don't think Prop. 64 goes far enough for restorative justice. But thank goodness there are industry leaders who brought this up or else we wouldn't have gotten anything at all.

Q: *When did you become a target for the Merced Police Department, and what has the experience been like? Does it affect your ability to do your job?*

A: I just lost a patient last week because, after legalization passed, they arrested me for having a tincture, which I made specially for that patient. They took that tincture and the thousands of dollars we had gathered in donations for another patient. The money and tincture are still being held in evidence, but I have not been charged with any crime in connection to them.

They arrested me outside the playhouse where my children perform in plays. They did it in front of my children. They also arrested me at my house but haven't pressed charges from that incident either. Now my children are so scared of police, they don't know what to do.

I have been charged with 26 counts of tax evasion, but I'm on a break from court until April. Even though the DA says I evaded taxes 26 times, I still haven't seen the evidence against me. My attorney called and said, "Don't bother coming to court, there's no discovery, they haven't presented me with anything to back up the 26 counts."

This is against me personally. My charity's 501(c)(3) status is solid, it's in compliance with everybody. You can go online and verify that. The D.A. charged me personally to make a splash in the paper, the same week that absentee ballots mailed out for the city council election. This litigation has been going on for a year. I have a constitutional right to a speedy trial, but I still haven't seen any evidence.

When I'm worried about fighting all of these legal battles, it wears on me. When I'm in court having to do all these things, I can't sufficiently focus on my patients to do the things that help them enhance their quality of life. Talk about financial ruin, two years ago we were treating cancer survivors for free, and we were able to fill the needs of every applicant. Then that changed. We had a garden for Lindsay, who's in hospice. We are a licensed garden, so we were cultivating for her to offset those costs. But those plants were destroyed by the cops, and she's in hospice right now because she decided she had become a financial burden on us.

My little sister was diagnosed with stage IV breast cancer last year. They said there would be no cure; I said hell no. I have been studying how to treat cancer for 10 years. I fired her oncologist, took her to Stanford, and we started a plant-based regimen of chemo plus herbs and cannabis to offset the effects of chemo. She was diagnosed in July and we started this in August. I noticed that the chemo was beginning to be detrimental. She had her first PET scan in November. All tumors had either shrunk or disappeared. The second PET scan in February showed the same results. Now, there is almost no evidence of tumor in her breast at all. If you let me do my job, we can save peoples' lives.

After all this, I'm still sitting in my office today, still open. If I did something wrong, why am I still here? I helped to write these laws, as president of the CCIA. I self-regulated prior to regulations being passed. I'm not trying to hide. And they have yet to win any court battles against me. They just arrest me to take my inventory and cash.

Q: *Based on your experience as a naturopathic doctor and an industry leader, what advice would you offer to state regulators facing decisions on how to implement these new rules?*

A: I would recommend that we remain cognizant of the quantity of raw material or concentrated versions that patients are allowed to have. That's the one area where my voice can have an impact. That, and making sure there are facilities available to provide the quality and consistency of cannabinoid profiles for patients. There are patients who need a specific type and specific dosages to maintain their quality of life. The state has to remember that the needs of patients are not defined by the limits set on recreational use—to make sure they're not killing people with legislation.

Works Cited

The Medical Marijuana Regulation and Safety Act of 2015 (MMRSA), consisting of:

▸ AB 243, now codified in Articles 6, 13 and 17 of Chapter 3.5 of the Business and Professions Code (Sections 19331 et seq., 19350 et seq., and 19360); Sections 11362.769 and 11362.777 of the Health and Safety Code; Section 12029 of the Fish and Game Code; and Section 13276 of the Water Code.

▸ SB 643, now codified in Sections 144, 19302.1, 19319, 19320, 19322, 19323, 19324, 19325, 19331, 19335 et seq., 19337 et seq., 19348, 2220.05, 2241.5, 2242.1, and 2525 et seq. of the Business and Professions Code.

▸ AB 266, now codified in Sections 27, 101, 205.1, and Chapter 3.5 (commencing with Section 19300) to Division 8 of, the Business and Professions Code; Section 9147.7 of the Government Code; Section 11362.775 of the Health and Safety Code; Section

147.5 to the Labor Code; and Section 31020 to the Revenue and Taxation Code.

The Adult Use of Marijuana Act of 2016 (AUMA or Prop. 64), now codified in Sections 11018 et seq. and 11357-11362.755 of the California Health and Safety Code; Sections 81000, 81006, 81007, 81008, and 81010 of the Food and Agricultural Code; Division 10 (Sections 26000-26211) of the Business and Professions Code; Section 147.6 of the Labor Code; Section 13276 of the Water Code; and Part 14.5 (commencing with Section 34010) of Division 2 of the Revenue and Taxation Code.

Judicial Council of California Criminal Jury Instructions section 16.831: http://www.courts.ca.gov/partners/documents/calcrim_2016_edition.pdf

California NORML's "Local Medical Marijuana Cultivation & Possession Guidelines in California."

http://www.canorml.org/medical-marijuana/local-growing-limits-in-California

Caulkins et al, *Marijuana Legalization: What Everyone Needs to Know, 2nd Edition. Oxford University Press, 2016.*

Caulkins et al, *Considering Legalization: Insights for Vermont and Other Jurisdictions.* RAND Corporation, 2015.

County by County

THE COMPLICATED LEGISLATIVE HISTORY OF MMRSA means that any list of marijuana cultivation bans in California must be taken with a grain of salt. In its final form at the time of its passage in 2015, the bill included a provision which seemed to imply that local governments would lose all ability to regulate cannabis cultivation to the state if they did not have their own ordinance in place by March 1st, 2016. MMRSA's author called this provision a "drafting error" and Governor Brown signed an emergency fix bill which repealed this controversial measure before the March deadline had passed; nevertheless, many panicked local governments rushed to pass temporary bans upon the advice of their government attorneys, in order to protect their ability to regulate in the future.

So auguring which counties may try to ban as much cannabis activity as possible under Prop. 64 and MMRSA is difficult, but this list is the best indication we have. Thanks to California NORML for doing most of the research I needed to compile it.

Alameda County
Regulated cultivation?: http://www.eastbaytimes.com/2017/01/16/alameda-county-lays-groundwork-for-marijuana-farms/
Bans manufacturing
Fremont: BAN
Oakland: regulation

Alpine County
Total BAN - http://cannabusinesslaw.com/2016/12/local-law-is-king-ten-counties-expressly-ban-medical-cannabis-businesses/

Amador County
12-plant limit
Bans manufacturing, commercial

Butte County
Regulates cultivation, bans manufacturing & commercial

Calaveras County
Gardens permitted with fees?
Manufacturing?
Regulated commercial

Colusa County
Total BAN—
http://cannabusinesslaw.com/2016/12/local-law-is-king-ten-counties-expressly-ban-medical-cannabis-businesses/

Contra Costa County
Total BAN—
http://cannabusinesslaw.com/2016/12/local-law-is-king-ten-counties-expressly-ban-medical-cannabis-businesses/

Del Norte County
Regulates cultivation, bans manufacturing & commercial

El Dorado County
Regulates cultivation & commercial; bans manufacturing

Fresno County
Total BAN—
http://cannabusinesslaw.com/2016/12/local-law-is-king-ten-counties-expressly-ban-medical-cannabis-businesses/

Glenn County
Regulates cultivation, bans manufacturing & commercial

Humboldt County
Regulating commercial, cultivation, manufacturing

Imperial County
Regulating cultivation, bans manufacturing & commercial

Inyo County
Regulates cultivation; bans manufacturing & commercial

Kern County
Regulates commercial; bans cultivation & manufacturing
Cities:
Bakersfield: BAN

Kings County
Total BAN - http://cannabusinesslaw.com/2016/12/local-law-is-king-ten-counties-expressly-ban-medical-cannabis-businesses/

Lake County
Commercial & cultivation regulation, bans manufacturing

Lassen County
Up to 72 plants
Bans manufacturing &
commercial

Los Angeles County
Total BAN—
http://cannabusinesslaw.
com/2016/12/local-law-is-
king-ten-counties-expressly-
ban-medical-cannabis-
businesses/
  Long Beach: regulation of ALL
  Los Angeles: regulation
  (Measure M)

Madera County
Regulates cultivation, bans
manufacturing & commercial

Marin County
Regulates cultivation &
commercial, bans
manufacturing

Mariposa County
Regulates cultivation, bans
manufacturing & commercial

Mendocino County
Regulates cultivation &
commercial, manufacturing
pending

Merced County
Regulates cultivation, bans
manufacturing & commercial

Modoc County
Regulates cultivation, bans
manufacturing & commercial

Mono County
Regulates cultivation, bans
manufacturing & commercial

Monterey County
Regulates cultivation,
manufacturing & commercial

Napa County
Regulates cultivation, bans
manufacturing & commercial

Nevada County
Outdoor cultivation ban; indoor
regulated. Initiative?
Bans manufacturing,
commercial

Orange County
Regulating cultivation, bans
manufacturing & commercial
Cities:
  Anaheim: BAN
  Irvine: BAN
  Santa Ana: regulations

Placer County
Total BAN—
http://cannabusinesslaw.
com/2016/12/local-law-is-
king-ten-counties-expressly-
ban-medical-cannabis-
businesses/

Plumas County
Cultivation bill introduced
Bans manufacturing &
commercial

Riverside County
Bans cultivation,
manufacturing, commercial
  Riverside city: commercial
  ban

Sacramento County
Regulates cultivation; bans
manufacturing, commercial

San Benito County
Regulates cultivation; bans
manufacturing & commercial

San Bernardino County
Bans cultivation,
manufacturing & commercial
San Bernardino city:
commercial regulation

Fontana: commercial ban, limited cultivation

San Diego County
Mostly BANs—SD City is regulating
Regulating cultivation, bans manufacturing & commercial
San Diego city: regulated retail; unknown cultivation, testing & manufacturing
Chula Vista: ban

San Francisco County
Regulating commercial, cultivation, manufacturing

San Joaquin County
Total BAN—
http://cannabusinesslaw.com/2016/12/local-law-is-king-ten-counties-expressly-ban medical-cannabis-businesses/
Stockton: commercial regulation

San Luis Obispo County
Regulates commercial; bans manufacturing; cultivation pending

San Mateo County
Regulates cultivation & commercial, bans manufacturing

Santa Barbara County
Bans cultivation, manufacturing & retail

Santa Clara County
Regulates cultivation, bans manufacturing & commercial
San Jose: bans retail and collectives

Santa Cruz County
Regulating commercial, cultivation, manufacturing

Shasta County
Partial ban; indoor cultivation regulated
Bans manufacturing & commercial

Sierra County
Regulates cultivation, bans manufacturing & commercial

Siskiyou County
Regulates cultivation & commercial, bans manufacturing

Solano County
Regulates cultivation, bans manufacturing & commercial

Sonoma County
Regulates cultivation & commercial, bans manufacturing

Stanislaus County
Total BAN—
http://cannabusinesslaw.com/2016/12/local-law-is-king-ten-counties-expressly-ban-medical-cannabis-businesses/
Modesto: Ban, but plans to consider regulation ordinance

Sutter County
Outdoor ban/indoor regulated. Bans manufacturing & commercial.

Tehama County
Regulates cultivation, bans manufacturing & commercial

Trinity County
Regulating cultivation, bans manufacturing & commercial

Tulare County
Regulates cultivation & commercial; bans manufacturing

Tuolumne County
Cultivation regulated, bans manufacturing & retail

Ventura County
Regulating cultivation, bans manufacturing & commercial
Oxnard: BAN on all activity

Yolo County
Regulating cultivation; bans manufacturing & commercial

Yuba County
Regulates cultivation & commercial, bans manufacturing

APPENDIX B

Notable California Marijuana Cases since 1996

People v. Trippet ■ **1997**   Held: Defendants charged with possessing and transporting marijuana may retroactively use the Compassionate Use Act of 1996 as a defense, even if their actions occurred before it became law.

Lungren v. Pero ■ **12/12/1997**   Held: The passage of the CUA did not legalize the sale of marijuana, regardless of whether for medical purposes or not for profit. Overturned by SB 420.

People v. Rigo ■ **1/21/1999**   Held: A physician's recommendation of medical marijuana obtained after an arrest for marijuana cultivation does not retroactively form a defense to the crime.

People v. Young ■ 9/13/2001   Held: A defendant transporting marijuana may not avail himself of the medical marijuana defense if he cannot show that the product is headed toward legitimate patients. Overturned by MMRSA.

People v. Fisher ■ 3/14/2002   Held: Law enforcement officers are not required to abandon a search for marijuana authorized by a search warrant when a resident of the premises to be searched produces documents that suggest he has a physician's permission to possess the marijuana.

People v. Mower ■ 7/18/2002   Held: The Compassionate Use Act (CUA) conveys a limited immunity against not only conviction but also arrest and other criminal proceedings in the absence of reasonable or probable cause of violation of the laws. Arrested defendants are entitled to a pre-trial hearing to determine this cause.

Conant v. Walters ■ 10/29/2002   Held: The federal government may not enjoin doctors in medical marijuana states from discussing or recommending marijuana to treat conditions, as opposed to prescribing a specific medical marijuana product.

People v. Jones ■ 9/30/2003   Held: Defendants in marijuana cases may call their doctor to testify to their medical use under the CUA.

People v. Tilehkooh ■ 12/8/2003   Held: Lawful use of marijuana in compliance with the CUA is not a probation violation, despite probation requirements to refrain from drugs and to obey the laws of the United States.

Bearman   v.   Superior   Court   of   Los   Angeles ■ 4/1/2004   Held: Courts may not subpoena patient records in their investigations into whether a doctor may have negligently recommended medical marijuana.

Gonzalez v. Raich ■ 6/6/2005   Held: The federal Controlled Substances Act remains supreme over state medical marijuana laws through the Commerce and Necessary and Proper clauses of the Constitution.

People v. Urziceanu ■ 9/12/2005   Held: The Medical Marijuana Program (MMP) created by SB 420 in 2003 creates a medical marijuana "collective defense" which can be applied retroactively. Overturned by MMRSA January 2018.

People v. Wright ■ 11/27/2006   Held: The SB 420 MMP created a retroactive immunity for the transportation of marijuana for a legitimate medical collective. Overturned by MMRSA January 2018.

People v. Mentch ■ 10/18/2006   Held: That defendants in marijuana cultivation cases have the right to a primary caregiver defense which also covers compensation for reasonable expenses related to cultivation, when the level of caregiving extended beyond mere cultivation to also include counseling and accompanying patients to doctor's offices.

People v. Strasburg ■ 3/22/2007   Held: The limited immunity granted to medical marijuana patients by state laws does not provide a shield against reasonable investigations and searches.

Garden Grove v. Superior Court ■ 11/28/2007   Held: Local governments must return marijuana seized during the investigation of a suspect after it is determined that the suspect is a valid patient in compliance with state medical marijuana laws.

People v. Chakos ■ 12/21/2007   Held: Absent any particular expertise in the lawful use of medical marijuana, the opinion of an arresting officer on the quantity of marijuana found is not sufficient to sustain a conviction for possession of marijuana with intent to sell.

People v. Hua ■ 1/11/2008   Held: A police officer's observation of people smoking marijuana inside a home is not sufficient for him to enter and conduct a warrantless search of that home.

Ross v. Raging Wire Telecommunications ■ 1/24/2008 Held: Under California law, an employer may require pre-employment drug tests and take illegal drug use into consideration in making employment decisions.

People v. Windus ■ 7/30/2008   Held: Possession and cultivation limits contained within SB 420's MMP do not curtail a patient or caregiver's rights under the CUA.

People v. Phomphakdy ■ 7/31-2008   Held: Possession and cultivation limits contained within SB 420's MMP are an unconstitutional restriction of CUA's constitutional guarantees.

County of San Diego v. NORML, et al. ■ 7/31/2008 Held: Provisions of the MMP requiring California counties to comply with the issuance of medical marijuana identification cards are not unconstitutional as violations of the federal Controlled Substances Act.

People v. Luna ■ 1/15/2009 Held: Mere planning or preparation to butane-extract marijuana concentrate not sufficient to uphold a conviction.

City of Claremont v. Kruse ■ 8/27/2009 Held: The operation of a medical marijuana dispensary without a business permit and license may be considered a public nuisance by a local government. Partly overturned by MMRSA/Prop. 64.

People v. Moret ■ 12/28/2009 Held: A probation restriction forbidding a recently enrolled medical marijuana patient from using marijuana is a proper exercise of court authority.

People v. Kelly ■ 1/21/2010 Held: Insofar as the MMP burdens a defense under the CUA to a criminal charge of possessing or cultivating marijuana, it impermissibly amends the CUA and in that respect is invalid.

Qualified Patients Association v. City of Anaheim ■ 2/18/2010 Held: The federal Controlled Substances Act does not prevent medical marijuana patient plaintiffs from challenging a local government ban on medical marijuana collectives on the basis that such a ban would violate the CUA and MMP.

People v. Colvin ■ **2/23/2012**   Held: Mere financial support from members of a legitimate storefront collective is sufficient to establish a collective defense under the MMP. Overturned by MMRSA January 2018.

People v. Jackson ■ **10/24/2012**   Held: The defense the MMPA provides to patients who participate in collectively or cooperatively cultivating marijuana requires that a defendant show that members of the collective or cooperative: (1) are qualified patients who have been prescribed marijuana for medicinal purposes, (2) collectively associate to cultivate marijuana, and (3) are not engaged in a profit-making enterprise. As we interpret the MMPA, the collective or cooperative association required by the act need not include active participation by all members in the cultivation process but may be limited to financial support by way of marijuana purchases from the organization. Overturned by MMRSA January 2018.

People v. Leal ■ **0/29/2012**   Held: Courts may restrict participation in the MMP as a condition of probation arising from a conviction for illegally selling marijuana and possession of a firearm.

Conejo Wellness Center, Inc. V. City of Agoura Hills ■ **3/29/2013**   Held: Local bans of medical marijuana collectives are not preempted by the CUA and MMP, because these laws do not create a "right" to medical marijuana. Partly overturned by MMRSA/Prop. 64.

City of Riverside v. Inland Empire Patients Health and Wellness Center, Inc. ■ **5/6/2013**   Held: California medical marijuana laws do not preempt local bans of collectives based on land use and zoning power. Partly overturned by MMRSA/Prop. 64.

Maral, et al., v. City of Live Oak ■ **11/26/2013**   Held: California's medical marijuana laws do not preempt the police power of local governments to ban marijuana cultivation. Partially overturned by MMRSA/Prop. 64.

People v. Baniani ■ **8/22/2014**   Held: The sale of medical marijuana is not illegal if it is within the context of a collective not-for-profit membership organized in compliance with the MMP. Overturned by MMRSA January 2018.

People v. Orlosky ■ **1/16/2015**   Held: The indicia of a formally organized collective is not a mandatory requirement that precludes application of the medical marijuana collective defense. Overturned by MMRSA January 2018.

Kirby v. Fresno ■ **12/1/2015**   Held: Local government land use authority to regulate or ban marijuana activity is not restricted by California's medical marijuana laws. Partially overturned by MMRSA/Prop. 64.

The Kind and Compassionate v. City of Long Beach ■ **7/12/2016**   Held: Local authority to regulate or ban medical marijuana collectives or activity is not preempted by state medical marijuana laws. Partly overturned by MMRSA/Prop. 64.

California's Marijuana law is constantly evolving and changing. Visit **Edrosenthal.com** for the latest information about California's New Rules.

NEW RULES

SPONSOR SECTION

Thank you to all the wonderful
companies whose support and
participation made this book possible.

TARANTULA

/təˈran(t)SHələ/
noun

 .... *INDOOR*

tarantula .... *OUTDOOR CLEAN GREEN CERTIFIED ORGANIC*

GANJA GOLD

1.   a rare, fire pre-roll comprised of the top 1% of lab-tested flowers, CO_2 wax, hash, and kief, rolled in raw natural paper. Emanating with a robust natural taste, these pre-rolls are exceptionally smooth and extremely potent. Tarantulas are exclusive, "one-of-a-kind" and made only by GanjaGold.

ORIGINAL

DISCREET

ANYTIME

STRENGTH

TRUSTED

BALANCE

CHEWS WISELY™
cheebachews.com

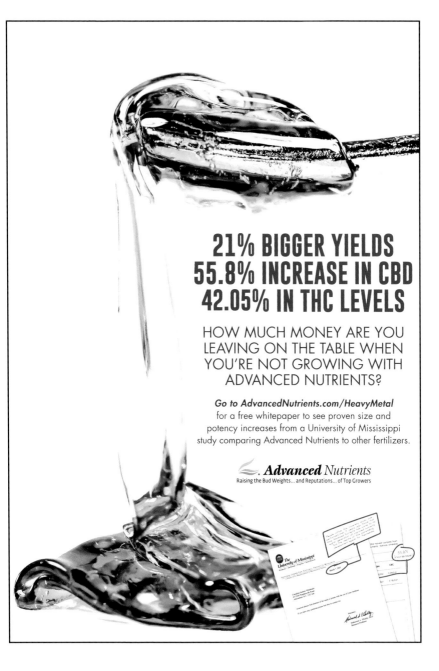